# Divinations: Four Plays

JOHN KINSELLA is the author of over twenty books, including *The Silo* (FACP, 1995), *The Undertow: New & Selected Poems* (Arc, 1996), *The Hunt* (Bloodaxe, 1998), *Visitants* (Bloodaxe, 1999), and *Wheatlands* (with Dorothy Hewett, FACP, 2000), *The Hierarchy of Sheep* (Bloodaxe/FACP, 2000/2001), and *Auto* (Salt, 2000). He is editor of the international literary journal *Salt*, a consultant editor of *Westerly* (CSAL, University of Western Australia), Cambridge correspondent for *Overland* (Melbourne, Australia), and international editor of the American journal *The Kenyon Review*. He is a Fellow of Churchill College, Cambridge University, Adjunct Professor to Edith Cowan University, Western Australia, and Professor of English at Kenyon College. *Peripheral Light: Selected and New Poems* is due out with W. W. Norton in 2003.

TRACY RYAN has published four full-length collections of poetry, most recently *Hothouse* (FACP, 2002), as well as two novels, *Vamp* (FACP, 1994) and *Jazz Tango* (FACP, 2002).

STEPHEN CHINNA teaches in theatre and performance studies, and scriptwriting, in English, Communication and Cultural Studies at the University of Western Australia. As part of his teaching and research activities he has written and/or directed numerous public theatre productions. He is the author of *Performance: Recasting the Political in Theatre and Beyond* (Peter Lang, 2003).

# Divinations

## Four Plays

## John Kinsella

*Edited by Stephen Chinna*

PUBLISHED BY SALT PUBLISHING
PO Box 937, Great Wilbraham PDO, Cambridge CB1 5JX United Kingdom
PO Box 202, Applecross, Western Australia 6153

© John Kinsella, 2003

PERFORMANCE
No performance may be given without a licence. Application for performance should be
made to the author's agent: Clive Newman, PO Box 2112 Kardinya WA 6163 Australia.

First published 2003

Printed and bound in the United Kingdom by Lightning Source

Typeset in Swift 9.5 / 13

ISBN 1 876857 66 8 paperback

SP

1 3 5 7 9 8 6 4 2

*For Tim Cribb who believes all the time,*
*even when he questions . . .*

# Contents

# A Gesture Towards a Poetics of Theatre

Of these four plays, three were written to be performed, and the fourth was written in response to a performance happening around me. One of the plays is a collaboration, so that's an occasion of mutual response. They are all, to varying degrees, "verse" plays, though the amount of verse varies considerably. All are written from a poet's perspective, and with an ear to colloquialisms as drama. Dance and movement across the stage are pivotal, as is light. Even if the manner of lighting is not indicated, the mood of the piece is a fair indication. Most significantly, I think, each was intended as a template for those who make things happen on the stage. They are to be pulled apart, workshopped, rewritten, re-articulated. They might be performed exactly as is, or in variation.

Each has an ethical intent, and I would hope this is respected, but that ethical intent itself is under scrutiny, so who am I to say. . . ? In fact, the premier performance of *Crop Circles* in Cambridge engendered that kind of debate: the "surrealism" and abstraction of the play, the use of myth and archetypes, against the realism and seemingly overt moral messaging. I would suggest the boundaries are far more blurred than this. Take these plays where you will. Maybe a brief mention of places and circumstances of composition will help.

*Crop Circles* came together from notes and poems and an idea of a story – thus, I suppose, it lends itself to being the most narrative of the plays. I sewed it together while on a residency at Varuna Writers' Centre, making use of the office computer late at night and in the early hours of the morning, in a removed and slightly threatening mindset. The play was revised later in Cambridge, and then workshopped at the Playbox with an excellent group of Australian actors under the direction of Aubrey Mellor. The dramaturgical assistance, and directorial input from the Playbox regulars, were eye-opening in terms of dramatic intent – of delaying a revelation to the last possible moment. Years of reading poetry aloud, and hearing others reading my poetry aloud, gave me a groundwork for projection of the colloquial and yet versified voice. I also had a map of relations and friends and people I had encountered in the Australian wheatbelt over the years to draw upon for tone and modulation.

The second play collected here, *Smith Street*, came about from living with my partner and co-writer Tracy Ryan on the notorious street of inner-city Perth frequented by prostitutes, and vilified by the government, police, and good citizens of the neighbourhood. As with the other plays, it is concerned with issues of bigotry and oppression, of hypocrisy and liberation. Heaven, Earth, and Hell are clearly delineated and the players are constantly struggling to preserve or dissolve these boundaries. It is a passion play. It's mystery, miracle, and morality rolled in together. Always elements of cabaret, melodrama and farce. In some senses, the closer to the "action", the more fantastical the "voicing" of the work. Steve Chinna, who directed the first production of this play at the University of Western Australia, also developed the script in a number of ways – primarily in the use of song. Smith Street was the realisation of the director using the script as template, and enhancing and giving a particular vision to the work.

The third play, *The Wasps*, was written specifically for the Cambridge Marlowe Society, though constructed in Ohio and Western Australia, as well as in Cambridge itself. I had enjoyed the Marlowe's interpretation of Australian spatiality in their production of *Crop Circles*, and sought to use what I'd learnt from this experience when writing Australian characters in a London setting in *The Wasps*. The centre cannot hold? And which centre, or centres? So the discourse goes . . . It is based on dance movement and light-play. Each of these plays works through a dramatic synaesthesia, with elements of sound and sight providing as much dramatic and "narrative" action as the storyline itself.

In writing *The Wasps*, with its obvious classical subtext (though ironised and displaced), I spent much time reading masques – Jonson (especially in the context of the dramatisations by Inigo Jones), Campion, Milton (textually) . . . The anti-masque as a form particularly interested me, and the literal writing of masques is what interests me in theatre at present. The influence on *The Wasps* isn't direct, but it's there – minimalised, distracted, and honed down. It's an undoing of the form, as one might almost expect; in the same way that *Smith Street* plays with the conventions of Victorian melodrama.

The last play here is described as "unperformable". Its place of composition was the old Railway Hotel in the city of Perth, Western Australia (supposedly the most isolated capital city in the world). This hotel was knocked down about ten years ago, in the early hours of the morning, against a council preservation order. Its propped-up facade, all that remained, stood there for years with its boarded-off disembodied allotment of prime city development space behind. The irony was fitting. The Railway was one of the roughest pubs in Perth, and a central place for the scoring of narcotics. Users would score in the pub, climb the staircase, and hit up in one of the guest bathrooms upstairs, often nodding off on the floor or in an empty bathtub.

What was remarkable about the Railway was that it was a meeting place for blacks and whites. There was the usual racism, but somehow brothers and sisters could be discovered across the divide of the pool table. Problems were, in some ways at least, shared. This part of the play speaks for itself. It's a play about respect and disintegration, and the entanglement of these in a city where the oppression of marginal groups – especially of those who might claim primacy over the land the State exploits – led to communication between those outside the machine, taking place in zones of the condemned.

There is little narrative action in *Paydirt*; the drama is in the words being spoken at all, and suggestion of things that have already happened. There is a sense of the Odyssey about it, but this is inverted. People drink and die, the dance goes on. The dance of constraint and oppression, but also of vision and connection with a place overlaid by the city, by the invaders. It's the common space, the meeting place, where in loss something is gained. I like to think of *Paydirt* as a distracted Miracle Play. This is the only play not to have been performed, or to be in preparation for performance. Could it be performed? I suppose I'd like to think so, but maybe not.

My influences as a young writer were, profoundly, Aeschylus, Sophocles, Euripides, Aristophanes, Beckett, Brecht (especially his play *Baal*: I wrote a play called *Baal* which has been lost), Shakespeare, and, indeed Marlowe and Goethe (textually), forgotten playwrights like Heywood (also my grandfather's surname), Indonesian shadow puppet theatre, anonymous Elizabethan plays in facsimile manuscript form (*The Wasps* actually gets its name from one of these), Dorothy Hewett, Jack Davis (a little later), and maybe Gertrude Stein. *Paydirt* is the inability to recognise the need to dramatise nothingness. The stage never stays still, and that's climax enough.

Strangely, *Paydirt* is filled with the most "real" of people, and yet they primarily act as ciphers in the play – static, people coming and going around a pool table, collecting drinks from the bar. Other than the main character Samuel, they come and go and become interchangeable. Samuel plays the prophet, but is not really up to the role fate and his own free will cast him in. He is a blind seer – but one whose blindness enhances seeing through sensitivity and an alternative sight. He stumbles through memories and glimpses of insight. His flaws overwhelm him. Samuel would have us think he alone is there, but so would each of the other characters if only we could see them as they would have us see them. But we can't, because we don't know how to look. Theatre is supposed to do this for us? I don't think so.

Dramatic action is built into language itself, and the compression and non sequiturs that vitalise poetry, that give it metaphoric resonance and metonymical links that become harder and harder to trace, are the rise and fall of movement for me. The actor takes us into the words themselves, as well as the meaning that comes from hearing the words spoken together. Maybe I am visualising a theatre in which we look and hear in a different way: we see something different because we want to. We are not passive, even when the players are apparently passive.

*Paydirt* was another lost play until a few years ago – it vanished for a decade and was found in my mother's shed. It was transcribed (with minor translation loss), and a small amount of additional material was added more recently. Its structure has not changed at all. Neither have the intentions and visualisations behind the piece, no matter how tempting this might be. I have decided not to collect my earliest plays – written almost twenty-two years ago – because, in some senses, they are a forerunner of these views of theatre. I think I became more amenable to the expectations of an audience to be entertained as I got older. I went to a great deal of theatre as a young man, and fed my plays with this very direct experience. They were conversations with and against convention, that remained determinedly introverted, dramatically, because most of what I had seen tried so hard to give people a good time. If people find this volume of interest, I expect those early plays will be transcribed from manuscripts (mostly hand-written and in archives), and presented for the reader, and maybe, maybe in the "right" hands, performed.

JOHN KINSELLA
November 2002

# A Marlovian Note on Divinations

In 1998 Cambridge University Marlowe Dramatic Society was privileged to give John Kinsella's play, *Crop Circles*, its premiere.

That conjuncture calls for comment. Why on earth should a British student drama society be chosen as vehicle for a play so profoundly rooted not just in Australia but in South Western Australia and in the Wheat Belt at that? The experiences it drew on and referred to, its fauna and flora, its idioms were way outside the ken of most of the company we assembled to tackle the project. I've given an account of the solutions we came up with in "Mind the Gap", a contribution to *Fairly Obsessive: Essays on the Works of John Kinsella*. Reading the four plays that together make up the present volume suggests some further reasons for this odd-couple marriage.

They derive partly from the character of one of the partners, the Marlowe (as it is known). It was founded in 1907 in reaction against the actor manager grand style in acting and overblown realist style in staging then dominant and specifically to tackle plays in verse by Shakespeare's contemporaries, at that time almost completely forgotten by the British stage. It was thus an experimental society which had to find out how to tackle the project it had set itself by what is, as Steve Chinna emphasises, ultimately the only way in theatre: simply by doing it – and finding out how to do poetry was a major part of doing it. That phase of the Society ran from 1907 to 1928 and the presiding spirit was Rupert Brooke's, although his dream of building a small experimental theatre in which the Marlowe could explore the contemporary German drama of Wedekind and others was never realised. From 1929 Dadie Rylands took over for a generation of productions until 1960. He redirected the Society's efforts towards

Shakespeare and these culminated in the recording of the complete works, the first ever, for Argo Records between 1957 to 1964. This was the school that nurtured the talents of John Barton, Peter Hall, who founded the Royal Shakespeare Company, and Trevor Nunn in directing, Ian McKellen and Derek Jacobi in acting. The emphasis on Shakespeare continued after Dadie's retirement until Sam Mendes's production of *Cyrano* in 1988, which inaugurated a return to the Society's founding principles, now extended to verse drama such as that of the Spanish Golden Age in addition to the Elizabethans. Since John Maynard Keynes had built the Arts Theatre in Cambridge in 1936 all the Marlowe's main productions had taken place there, that is, they were student productions but in a fully professional theatre. Alas, the return to experimental productions proved unviable at the box office and was abandoned in 1999, since which year the Society has returned to Shakespeare, working extensively with schools.

This is where John Kinsella comes in again. In 1998 he had founded an annual prize for students and followed this in 1999 with The Other Prize, to be awarded for a new play written by a student, and adjudicated by the Literary Manager of the RSC. (John is currently founding yet a third prize, The Komus, for musical composition setting text for theatre.) Part of the prize was to be a production of the winning text by the Marlowe in a small student theatre. Thus the Society is now committed to two productions a year, a main house production of Shakespeare at the Arts Theatre, and a small house production of new writing, and in the latter returns to its origins in finding out how to tackle the untried and the unknown. John's own play, *Crop Circles*, can be seen as inaugurating this new departure.

At the time the Marlowe was working on *Crop Circles*, *Paydirt* had been lost, forgotten, and was only discovered by John's mum in an outbuilding while we were in production. Furthermore, drafts of earlier plays are held in library collections as pointed out in the Notes to the Preface.

Reading it now in series with the plays that followed is illuminating. John's "Preface" mentions the influence of *Baal*, which is plain to see. Brecht's own introductory prologue to the 1918 version says that "The subject of this play is a very ordinary story of a man who sings a hymn to summer in a grog-shop without selecting his audience". To jump to a much later Brecht – of *The Caucasian Chalk Circle* –

Samuel in *Paydirt* is also an Azdak, a working-class and dissident intellectual in a downtrodden sector of Perth. The scenography is that of the cabaret, the poetics that of social epiphanies. But unlike *Baal* the play never moves into Nature; its space is confined to the bar and the alleyway just outside. That is what changes so strikingly in *Crop Circles*, where the spaces expand and natural forces, working through the varying resistances of the characters, become the main agents of the play. Hence the return to the urban in *Smith Street* is on terms different from *Paydirt*. Not only space but form is opened out by the brilliant device of incorporating a Medieval Morality scenography with the stereotypes of nineteenth-century melodrama. Relieved of the ambivalence and atmospherics that haunt *Paydirt*, the verse is released into wit and the tone lifts into comedy – indeed, at the beginning of Act 3 Angel anticipates the modality of *The Wasps* and begins to dance. With *The Wasps* we enter Pinterland (though further down river) where the banalities of urban living are invested with a dimension of fear and violence that cannot be identified but wells up in the pauses. When Dadie Rylands saw his first play by Pinter he recognised him as a poet of the theatre. John has taken that subtext and precipitated it into the music and dances that periodically take over and possess the characters. Act 3 may move into the de-historicised warehouse conversions and penthouses of Thatcher's Docklands, but the Thames, Conrad's river of darkness, still flows outside and early in the scene the lights reflected onto the ceiling from its waters begin to swirl. It is a comedic *danse macabre*.

This is the play that the Marlowe will explore, under the guidance of Steve Chinna, in some workshops early in 2003. With *Crop Circles* we could see the difficulty of exploring what seemed an alien landscape; *The Wasps* seems closer to home: beware!

TIM CRIBB
January 2003

## Rough Guides and Mutations:
## The "Difficult" Plays of John Kinsella

John Kinsella is, among many other manifestations, a poet, a novelist, an autobiographer, an academic, and a playwright. While not attempting to collapse, nor separate these roles, it is his plays – understandably, given the content of this volume – that will be my area of focus.

What is a play? It is not these words on the pages you will soon read – if you haven't already skipped this introduction and got to the real reason you have picked up this book. A play takes place in space and time, as does reading, but plays are collaborative hybrids of whatever intentions the participants may have, and whatever accidents may occur in their making. The play scripts you read here, are parts of plays. In his "Preface", John Kinsella says each play is a template – or, a pattern, a gauge, a guide – "for those who make things happen on the stage". Amongst multiple definitions, in the biological version a template is the molecular pattern governing the assembly of a protein – that is – an organic compound. If we leave aside poststructuralist quakings about the notion of the organic society – and the "Greenie" version of the "natural" or the "biodynamic" – and think of the organic as relating to a bodily organ or structure – then we may think of the accidental and the arbitrary, the fluctuations that disturb the smooth running of the whole. And if we continue with this organic metaphor – this molecular pattern is always potentially chaotic, and liable to mutation. Such mutation is instrumental in theatre work, where re-articulation through repetition drives the metaphoric engine of a play's workshopping, rehearsing, and production.

Kinsella's plays disturb the complacency of static positions concerning play structure, content, and form. Like all good plays, they present challenges. They challenge the actor or director who might wish for a smooth generic style. They challenge the actor who may want more information to help their psychologically motivated character evolve through a process of learning the great lessons of life – from the bottom to the top – or from triumph, descending through hubris in a tragic spiral downwards towards oblivion. They will challenge the actor or director who finds the shifts between prose and verse difficult to justify in terms of "realism" – whatever that may mean. The actor who can "sing" the poetry of the lines – whether prose or poetry – will fare better than the actor who must find a justification for those shifts. They will challenge those spectators who like their theatre palatable in the linearity of its form, and the familiarity of its narrative. They also will challenge those who shy away from the overtly political, or even polemical – believing that postmodern means post-Brechtian – and the declamatory wearing of one's ecological or anarchist heart on one's sleeve bespeaks a certain "uncool" approach to a politics of the cynical snigger and the shoulder shrug. While "social conscience" has a hernia-like ring to it – Kinsella's "social conscience" is informed by his position as a self-proclaimed anarchist. Not the anarchist of popular perception – who mutters that "the system's fucked, mate" or else throws bombs at Archdukes, but the anarchism of the self-reflective, self-motivated political practitioner who believes that a situational, contextual, small-group politics of protest can have a small "p" – and manifest itself in performance without regard for generic and/or generational fashions in acceptable activism.

These plays are unabashed in their use of "local" knowledges. Kinsella writes of his environment in his poetry, and his plays. It is the environment of the wheatlands, the "scrub", the bush, and the small towns of rural Western Australia. It is also the environment of inner-city Perth – where prostitutes and their clients, cops and politicians, journalists and vigilantes can make mileage and more from what may be designated as crime; where the junkies and boozers and the people off the mainstream road trade in love, drugs, dreams, and aspirations on the bitumen and paving slabs, and in the dark, cool front-bars of the "seedier" parts of the city. This is Australian theatre – but that term is as nebulous as "British", or "American" theatre. It is not universal – the events are circumscribed by local knowledges, local politics, local lifestyles, and local author-ity. But, this is not a defiantly Australian theatre – there is no axe to grind to find an "Australian voice". That battle was fought in the 1960s and 1970s. Whether it was won or lost is, in some ways, immaterial. While these plays, in the main, are assertively "local", they are – assertively – plays that can and will travel.

Kinsella sees theatre as "a poetic space". He asks rhetorically, in an interview with Rod Mengham in *Fairly Obsessive*: "which IS closer to thought ... speech or writing? Or the space of the theatre?" (Mengham and Phillips, 286). While it appears no clear answer is forthcoming, there is an answer – theatre allows the opportunity for spaces, lacunae, in the spoken words – visible and visceral punctuations in the flow of language, where stasis is foresworn, and the poetics of human motion can work in harmony, or counterpoint, to the declamation of the voice. But, these plays do not "flow" – if flow implies a seamless rhythm based on a classical form. The flow here is more atonal – more Stockhausen than Strauss. It is the sound of the true discord of the "real" – rather than of the wishful desire for the eventual accord of Naturalism and the well-made play. There is an element of the "musical" in all of these plays – that sometimes seemingly awkward bursting into verse, or song, that Naturalism killed with its attention to "reality". Of course, in "real life" we are never poetic, and we never sing.

The title of the collection is *Divinations*. Here we have invocations of a sublime – the unpresentable of the supernatural (where the "natural" – ever unnatural – looms large in its own invocations). Through an ever unnatural/natural foreseeing, or foretelling, which is not programmatic, these plays sort through the entrails of societies to divine the future through the present.

*Crop Circles* was first performed at Cambridge in 1998, in a Marlowe Society production directed by Tim Cribb. The play is dedicated to Dorothy Hewett, an inspirational Western Australian writer, poet, playwright, and political activist. Like John Kinsella, she is a poet who "speaks" from the wheatlands. Her plays have invariably been seen as problematic, for their politics in part, but especially for their style. Hewett mixes genres – she is not concerned with stylistic purity, and like Kinsella, happily mixes the naturalistic with the surrealistic, the prosaic with the poetical, and moves into song and dance with a specific and entertaining political value.

This play deals with a central issue in much of rural Australia – salinity – where due to over-zealous land clearing, and poor land management, the water table has risen, pushing up the underlying salt (deposited when much of the Australian land mass lay under the oceans). This has rendered much of the always marginal arable land unfit for crops or grazing, and belated efforts are now being made to revegetate the farmlands, and educate people in more responsible land management. This ecological disaster may be put down to greed, ignorance, or – perhaps – even a baleful chthonic vengeance against the usurpation and degradation of the landscape. But, while the "underworld" may be seeking revenge, or justice, a pragmatic and emblematic sign is also scarring the landscape. Crop circles – even fake – have an air of the theatrical about them. Whether their making is performed by tractor, "round up", or carnivalesque bodies under the harvest moon – or by extraterrestrial landing craft – they have a certain ludicrous (from *ludicrum* – stage play) quality – as playful as the debate that is generated by their appearances throughout "civilized" nations. Here, they have a commercial quality – as potential tourist attraction – as well as being a catalyst for social action by the marginalised against yet another manifestation of a long line of robber barons – in the character of Sayers. Spatially, the division of the stage into the white, salt-blasted lands of the "wheatbelt", and the green, over-fertilized fields of Sayers, sets up a binary which is mediated by a place from which to speak – whether it be the Town Hall, the raised lookout, or a farmhouse. For a very pertinent director's point-of-view on this play, see Tim Cribb's essay "Mind the Gap: John Kinsella's Verse Drama," in *Fairly Obsessive* (Mengham and Phillips, 221–34).

*Smith Street* had its first production at the Dolphin Theatre, the University of Western Australia, in May 2001. This play grew – or mutated – from a collaboratively written script by John Kinsella and Tracy Ryan. It was sent to me with a generous open invitation to do what I would with it: to add material, and to workshop it for performance. The performers helped shape the play, as did the crew. As does the set, the venue, the lighting, the available technology, the music choices . . . and not least – the spectators. So too did Anna Brockway, a theatre practitioner, who helped teach the student actors much about the possibilities of stage movement, and stage pictures. John attended one rehearsal, sitting still and silent in the background – freely giving over his "rights" to interruption or intervention. Indeed, when student participants asked him what he thought, his response was to decline comment – other than being encouraging about their performances. Not "his" play – as an entity – but his play in part, as a collaboration between writers, practitioners, and – importantly – the process.

*Smith Street* might be seen as a simple clash – a classical conflict between the forces of law and order – the politicians, the police, the "wowsers" who seek out deviation, but manage to be spies, voyeurs, as well as thieves of pleasure – versus those who live outside the law. But, it is not that simple – thankfully – and there is more than enough ambiguity here to satisfy those who like their folktales to be less than specific in terms of judicially ordained "right" and "wrong". This "melodrama" – perhaps – plays type against type, interweaving a hybridity of inner-suburban street-life, with elements of farce and the nativity play – among other things. Is it a difficult play? It would appear so, judging on responses from participants and spectators alike. But, for those who enjoy difficulty, and do not aspire to an imagined generic, stylistic, thematic purity, then "difficulty" has a positive tone. Furthermore, the quarrel between the transparent and the opaque is no longer such an issue in academic discourses, with the understanding that these are reliant on subjective and contextual positionings – and we may all move at different times between our reception and interpretation of one or the other. For example, in the Dolphin production, slides of Mrs Walpurgis dressed as a prostitute were shown on the wall of the "Tuscan Splendour" at certain points – a not so subtle exposure of a potential secret life – but perhaps too subtle, in that spectators did not appear to connect the corporeality of the actor as Mrs Walpurgis on stage, with the image of the same actor as "prostitute".

Actors as well as spectators had difficulty deciphering some of the verbal imagery – as did this director at times. But, so what? It is not the business of the playwright/s to be transparent, and how can there ever be transparency for all? Is it necessary to know that certain prisons around Perth are named for local flora – Casuarina, Hakea, etc.? Perhaps . . . Towards the end of the play, Jack disappears, muttering mysteriously about "rehabilitation" and "parole". But, as Jack has earlier warned – "I'll be back" – and there is something of Jack and other protagonists from *Smith Street* in the characters of an earlier play – *Paydirt* – but more on that soon.

But, perhaps *The Wasps*, could be "read" as almost too transparent – starting as a seemingly naturalistic domestic scene of Shirley and Bill, inhabiting the "real" olde England, as colonials in search of magical answers, and job satisfaction. Beware. Kinsella doesn't write like this – and the marked banality of the dialogue between Shirley and Bill quickly shifts to other modes. And, in performance this seeming banality can be even more quickly destabilized through the actors' voices and movement. I reiterate – what you see on the page is not a performance. Get past the play as prose – envision its potentials as performance. This is how Kinsella writes – with a visual feeling, an aural sensitivity, and the rhythmic consciousness of a poet.

Intertextuality – as another academic discourse – is a given. If this play raises resonances of other plays – even through its title alone – these are necessary borrowings. We are indeed informed by what we are exposed to, and if Kinsella says elsewhere that Beckett is a "favourite" (*Fairly Obsessive*, 286), then we may well include as inspirations – among many – Ionesco, and Burroughs – especially in the figure of Stan the Exterminator. It is not my brief, nor desire, to supply "readymades" for interpretative analysis. As I have stated – perhaps interminably – to decipher plays from the page is a pointless exercise. How they pan out in rehearsal and performance, and how individual spectators interpret them, is where any interpretative value resides. This play will be yet another collaboration – between writer, director, choreographer, musical director, lighting, sound, actor and spectator. In a sense, how can we label any play writing as a solo effort – except that with copyright, and ascribed authorship, we must necessarily do so? And besides, how willing are any of us to relinquish our autonomous authority over our texts? It takes a generosity of spirit to do so – and Kinsella proves time and again that this is how he is prepared to work.

The playwright labels *Paydirt* as "unperformable". Is that a challenge? Most certainly. *Pace* the playwright, but this play is eminently performable. Here, in the earliest composed of these plays, the interweaving elements of voice, music, dance, and movement are evident.

As is that proclivity to generic hybridity – where cops can do dance routines, music can be "heard", but not heard, and where the spiritual can intertwine with the corporeal. For some, these will be vignettes of a recognizable life. Here, there is neither the space nor the need to give a history of the puritan constraints within Australian society – on the way that pleasure is defined, measured and controlled by a vocal minority of censors and vigilantes – the Clipboards and Walpurgis's of the suburban verges. Even more tellingly, behind the larrikin insouciance of the popular construct of the Australian (white, male, working class) lies an abiding conservatism that reacts swiftly and defensively to difference – in accent, dress, politics, sexual choices, etc. The Australian challenge – "What are ya?" – has always had a threatening subtext which signals fear, and a repression of deviance from the norm – the Anglo-Celtic masculinised Australian, of whatever gender.

But, contextually, for *Paydirt*, it is enough to say that licensing laws have only relatively recently loosened up – and it is not unusual a requirement to have to order a meal in order to obtain an alcoholic drink at many cafes. But, while a certain bohemian decadence might be the fiction of sitting about at 7am drinking cold beer – or tequila sunrises – the reality is more as *Paydirt* suggests – a bone-cold time of day with the smell of cigarette smoke and beer-filled carpets – and for some, sausage and egg and a cold beer at 6.30 in the morning, after having been up all night – spaced out, wasted – and somewhat hysterical.

Some years ago: "Where is the reality?" called a passing motorist to a companion and I as we roamed the streets of suburbia later one morning after a night of increasing dementia – and breakfast and drinks at an "early opener". I can't recall how we responded – other than with equally existential calls. But, they wanted the realty office – it was a mispronounced real estate quest. A surrealistic call and response on a hot summer morning, and the prosaic and the poetic are likewise entwined in *Paydirt*. This is not glamorous – it's hard and spacey in its "reality" – as the play moves skilfully between the arcane and the everyday.

But, to return to the label of the "unperformable". Perhaps that lies in the casting. Kinsella states that the play was written with the Nyungar actor, David Ngoombujarra in mind. Furthermore, that the ethnicity, or race/colour of the performers is non-specific, and that rather these are labels, or epithets, which may be ascribed to them, or directed at them. This is where the sensitivity lies – in who may perform an embodied "Aboriginality" in the visceral space of the theatre – but the "experiment" would be well worthwhile. However, while the boundaries of staging are "fluid", the reception may be less so. Nonetheless, to paraphrase Brecht: Let's see how it works in practice.

These are plays for performance. I won't stop returning to this. Some may think: "Oh no! He's not going to go on again about page to stage; text as performance, and so on". But yes – I will – even if not in so many words. The playwright has spoken of these plays in his author's preface; I have written briefly of them here. But whatever the author says, and whatever I say, will be of peripheral import to those who take these words and dis-place them to real space and time, with the breathing, moving bodies of performers, and crew, and spectators. There they will find their own particular forms, shifting through the process of rehearsal and workshopping to a process of performance, a performance in front of – or perhaps among – particular spectators, in a specific venue. *Crop Circles* will never be the same play/s as performed at the Wolfson Theatre, Churchill College, Cambridge; *Smith Street* will never be the play/s that were performed at the University of Western Australia; and when *The Wasps*, and *Paydirt*, are performed, their manifestations – mutations – in specific spaces and times, with specific participants, will continue to shift and change. Evolve is not a word to use here.

Read them for their poetry, read them for their explorations of form; read them for their occasional lapses as well as triumphs – why should John Kinsella be different to any other mortal? But above all (you knew I was coming to this) read them as performance potentials – as templates, recipes, star maps – rough guides scattered across the page/stage for your divination.

STEVE CHINNA
December 2002

# Crop Circles

*for Dorothy Hewett*

*A play in five acts*

Crop Circles was first performed by the Marlowe Society at the Wolfson Theatre, Churchill College, Cambridge, on October 20, 1998 with the following cast

| | |
|---|---|
| LEN | Nick Harrop |
| JO | Anna Mackenzie |
| GARY | Dave Allen |
| CLEM WRIGHT | Kevin Trainor |
| MARY WRIGHT | Tania King |
| SAYERS | Charlie Beall |
| LUCY | Annalisa D'Inella |
| DR CINDY EVANS | Sophie Levy |
| THE DIVINER | Steve Watts |
| MINISTER | John Finnemore |
| THE GREENIE | Douglas McCabe |

Directed by Tim Cribb.
Workshop and Mask Consultant by Roddy Maude-Roxby.
Produced by Alex Godden and Hattie Truscott.
Music composed by Jeremy Thurlow.
Set designed by Philip Clarke.
Lighting designed by Edward Ratzer.

Props and costumes by Catherine Firth.
Set built by Castle Associates.
Publicity by Rachel Flowerday.
Programme arranged by Stephanie Jones.
Photography by Dan Chastney.

## Characters

LEN, *journalist with a city newspaper. Early thirties. Reasonably successful, regarded as reliable. Slightly refined accent, though obviously Australian. A slight "rural" twang. But travelled and "worldly-wise". His family on his father's side is from Green Springs, but he hasn't seen them in over two decades.*

JO, *freelance photographer. Highly regarded landscape photographer. Late thirties. Part Nyungar. Fostered at a young age in suspicious circumstances. Apparently indifferent, but when roused capable of great passion. Informed, particular in her craft.*

GARY, *Gazzer to his mates. Mid twenties. Well-built shearer. Heavy drinker, shooter, party boy. But smart. And when not acting the clown, capable of penetrating insight. The local wit.*

[UNCLE] CLEM WRIGHT, *farmer. Stalwart in his 60s. Tries to follow the new ways. A mixture of old and new values. Gnarled and large.*

MARY WRIGHT, *conservationist, ex-schoolteacher.*

[ANDY] SAYERS, *Green Springs's largest landowner. Drives a Statesman. Power-hungry bigot, and misogynist.*

LUCY, *hobby farmer.*

DR CINDY EVANS, *local Doctor and first woman town mayor. "Conservationist", elected out of desperation. The town is dying from rising salinity.*

THE DIVINER, *figure of the Apocalypse.*

MINISTER, *Old England, dark and foreboding.*

GREENIE, *narrator.*

# The set

*The set should be projected onto a diorama if possible. The primary effect will be one of contrasts. The sky will be incredibly blue, the wheat fields, florescent green, the ready-to-harvest crops golden. The salt will be stark white. The central façade will vary from scene to scene. It will start as the façade to the Town Hall. The left side of the Town Hall will be stark white and blue, representing salinity and endless sky. The right side of the Town Hall will be green and blue, representing lush crops and sky. These will vary according to the stage directions.*

*Lighting should be such that it plays against the hues of the set. It should reflect the subtle moods of the day. In those scenes where environmental or moral equivocation is being focussed on, the light will be harsh, unforgiving.*

*Costumes should reflect the employment of the wearer.* CINDY *will be smart but casual, the shearer in a red checked shirt and/or a blue singlet, always wearing a pair of greasies.* LUCY *will be dressed butch, though with a touch of the "femme" about her.*

*It is essential for the actors to speak their "straight" lines in the same way they speak the poetry. And vice versa. In a sense this is one long poem in which they are manifestations of the spoken word. The distinction between character and language should be blurred. They are what they speak. The poetry and dialogue should be treated as one.*

# Act 1

## Scene 1

*Folk are emerging from double doors. These are the doors of the hundred-year-old Town Hall. In fact it is Green Springs's Centenary year and there are insipid reminders of this posted on the walls of the Town Hall's façade. As they make their way onto the street the* GREENIE's *opening "speech" is heard. He speaks from the "green side", but is lost in the halflight of the stage's periphery. Eventually* CINDY *and the* WRIGHTS *emerge, deep in conversation. They stand to one side, behind them the stark salt wastes spread into nothingness, cut only by the agonizingly blue sky. On the other side of the Town Hall it is lush and green. These are the lands of* ANDY SAYERS. *The* MINISTER *emerges and stays with his back to the brilliant greens. Black shoes, trousers, jacket, white shirt with cleric's collar. He has his hands crossed in front of him and is glowering in the direction of* CINDY *and her companions; it is obvious he despises them. As if sensing his animosity they simultaneously turn and glance at him before returning to their conversation. The crowd vanishes, and the* MINISTER *slowly walks into the wings.*

GREENIE

Down off the shoulder of the pink granite scarp
down in the rich soil where the roots run deep

crop circles appear with mathematical precision –
archetypal patterns that keep us wondering.

It's said they followed the people
from the Old Country – even after

the first clearing there was talk
of them, recurring every now and again

when the signs were right – when the harvest
was still some way off but the stems

of the long wheat varieties were fully
grown and the florescence of the crops

was at its peak. When the evenings
brooded bruised and red.


*We pick up the conversation between* CINDY *and the* WRIGHTS.

WRIGHT

Crop circles, what a load of rubbish. I reckon Sayers is up to something. I reckon he's been out there with some round-up and a length
of string. Soon the place will be crawling with cityfolk come to gawk
at his "visitation".

CINDY

Yeah, there's something suspect about it. Sayers is the most sceptical
man I've ever met – his conversion is a bit sudden. If it had been on
someone else's land he'd say it was a case of round-up and a piece of
string. I've heard he's got a reporter coming up from the city.

WRIGHT

It's the fact that he won't let anyone near it that bothers me. Standing
on his lookout and looking down at God knows what.

MARY

There's something about it, though.

CINDY

Well, it'd make a good photograph.

MARY

Yes, and I guess it isn't going to help with our problem much. The
salinity has almost reached the point of no return, but we've got to
convince them that it's not too late to take action.

CINDY

It's education that's needed. Any chance of typing that leaflet up tonight?

MARY

No problem.

CINDY

If you can do that I'll print it up and circulate it in the next couple of days. Make sure it includes all that information from the Ag Department about tree planting and contour banks. And if you could point out that the next meeting of the Land Committee will be held in chambers. Submissions to be made by the first of the month. The next general meeting will be in the Town Hall on the 15th.

WRIGHT

[*Monomaniacally.*] Crop circles! It's too much. And that bloody meteorite! Conveniently crashing into his paddock.

MARY

Let it go, Clem, it'll only eat away at you.

WRIGHT

Too bloody right it will! [*Hesitates and kicks at the ground, muttering*] . . . well, I've got to get back. The barometer's down and rain's coming. It'll bring more salt to the surface. The gulleys around the top paddock are still clogged. I want to clean the bottlenecks away, don't want a flood.

In the salt encrusted gulleys
silt drains to the deeper troughs
before being flushed out
by the winter wash.
In summer sheep
will stray through fences
& in search of water
will sink to their bellies
& stick, drowning
in those heatwaves

that roll across the shores
of such territories, silt
a kind of temporal
limbo.

Yeah, I'd better get back to it. You ready, Mary?

MARY

Yes. Well, we'll say our farewells, Cindy. Are you still okay for dinner
on Thursday night?

CINDY

Wild horses . . . [*She laughs.*]

GREENIE

Soon they'll come from the Post
and the Truth, the West Australian

and the local gazette, along with skeptics
and a brace of quacks all armed

with charts and instruments,
with metal detectors that transform

slivers of steel from a plough disc
into a discourse,

the weight of the heavens
now sits in fields as the salt

wells up and poisons
the fields.

*Fade out.*

## Scene 2

*Still outside the Town Hall. The* WRIGHTS *have left but* CINDY *is on her hands and knees gathering scattered sheets of paper. Her briefcase is open and she is stacking the documents into it.* GARY *saunters past and stands, legs apart, hands on hips, between her and the audience.*

GARY

Dropped something, Doc?

CINDY

Hello, Gary.

GARY

You wouldn't want to do that when you've got a scalpel in someone's guts. [*He crouches down next to her, towards the audience, and mockingly imitates an operation.*]

CINDY

[*Continuing to pick up papers, though slowly now, unfazed by* GARY'*s antics.*] You'd better watch out I don't slip next time I've got to stitch you up!

GARY

Yeah, I will. [*He grins and picks up a paper, scrutinizing it.* CINDY *motions to take it off him but thinks again and smiles.*]

CINDY

So, you can read!

GARY

Nah, I'm just trying to make an impression.

CINDY

Well, you've won me. [*She regrets saying this straight away.*]

GARY

Great! Let's go back to my caravan then.

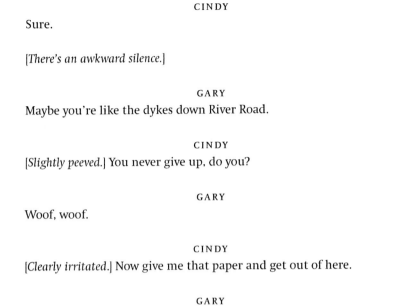

CINDY

Sure.

[*There's an awkward silence.*]

GARY

Maybe you're like the dykes down River Road.

CINDY

[*Slightly peeved.*] You never give up, do you?

GARY

Woof, woof.

CINDY

[*Clearly irritated.*] Now give me that paper and get out of here.

GARY

[*Holding the paper in front of her.*] Come on, now beg for it, beg for it.
Gazzer wants the bitch to beg.

CINDY

You're wasting your time here, buddy . . . [*sarcastically*] shouldn't you be
on guard duty for your mate Sayers? [GARY *drops the paper and saunters off.*]

*Fade out.*

## Scene 3

*The salt side of the stage is illuminated.* WRIGHT *is looking out onto the audience. He's shovelling silt from a gulley. He's speaking to himself with the
rhythm of the shovel strokes.* MARY *is in the background planting trees.*

WRIGHT

white-tailed black cockatoos
have given up their fly pasts

[17]

and the red-capped parrots
are crushed by cars and trucks,
the trees dying as the salt spreads
like gall insects just under the surface
the elusive night heron
with the weight of the old world
on its hunched shoulders
roosting primaeval during
the bright light of day
will prowl the dwindling swamps,
its ethereal visitation
doubly camouflaged

MARY

sometimes out rabbit-shooting
they'll catch a night heron
in their spotlight, set like wood
it dares them to lay down
their guns and return the night
to its silent hunters

WRIGHT
[Turning to MARY, almost connecting with her.]

remember the old house on the back road,
verandah so close to the road that its uprights
were marked with red reflectors,
the gate coming off the porch
onto red gravel threading towards the ranges ...
where a child stepped into the path
of a semi laden with grain at harvest
twenty years ago to the season,
the bloody gums cowering in the twilight,
as the open fields sank into the creek

MARY

[Quietly.] & blue-faced heron
ghosted the neglect ...

WRIGHT *wipes his brow, leans on his shovel then lays it down. He whistles to himself and then starts carving circles in the crusty salt surface.*

WRIGHT

[*Muttering to himself.*] Bloody crop circles. Water water everywhere, nor any drop to drink . . . Ridiculous. This place was once covered in lush crops, and before that thick scrub. We've territorialized it. The machines have cut the shadows' shape out and ground it to a paste. A salty paste. Even the fence posts dissolve, wire erodes. But slowly we're surrounding it with trees. Encircling it. Closing in. I've been fighting this bloody salt for twenty years. Two decades of warfare.

There's no salvaging the fruit-box,
nails already skeletons when the wood's
decomposition begins, nor the beer bottle ringed
corrosively. There's no salvaging a tableau
that's blank, nor foxprints overlaid
with ice drier than a saltbush's skin.
And there's no salvaging a prayer
breached when tides of faith falter
and the homestead collapses, when the flightless
nomads of the gullies rise up and conquer.

MARY

[*Staring out at the audience.*]

But even out there things live.
The fox will set his den deep in the salt
his prints pressed into the glassy surface.
Out there it's safe. A brace of top-notch pigeons
erupts as the fox noses the evening air.

WRIGHT

[*Muttering to himself.*]

The boody rat warrens stripped bare.
The fox moves through the paddock

of the Killers – those four lone sheep,
culled from the dwindling flocks.

*Sunset.*

## Scene 4

*The* GREENIE *speaking on the steps of the Town Hall. Most of the townsfolk
are standing around, looking up at him on the soapbox. He finishes his speech
and is both applauded and jeered.*

GREENIE
At a time when the less ecologically-minded
took to the salt lakes in farm utilities,
spotlights melting the salt's cold ice,
carving channels without style, the salt
foaming in crests, saltbush like storm-
ravished ships, mizzen masts driven
into the thick muddy swell, hooded
plovers moving frantically up to the stubble
as if this was all that was left of instinct,
when amber bullets rained down
onto the surface of the rising water-table
to be picked up like barnacled wreckage
decades later, & chemicals were poured
into cracks opened by earthquakes,
there remained the security that drought
or flood or destruction by unseasonal
storms was part of the idyll – you had
to take the good with the bad,
and as long as the yield averaged
out over the years – the treeless fields
responding to a new brand
of fertilizer – & the floor price
of wool remained fixed, stuff
the worry, isn't that it? So, there's
no point asking what I'm getting at

because it's all around you and who's heard
of a heatwave in the middle of winter
anyway?

[*From the crowd we hear "Piss off!"*]

Okay, I'll buy my own drinks.

### SAYERS

[*To* GARY *and anyone else who can hear.*] A bloody great ball of fire has
come out of the sky and this dopey bastard is wondering why it's hot.

### GARY

Bloody ear-bashing from another feral. "Shoot Ferals!" is what the
bumper sticker says, and if I could get away with it, that's exactly what
I'd do. A good blast from the old Ruger right between the eyes. Dazzle
him with the spotlight and he'd be up on his hind legs, paws limp in
front of his chest, and [*feigning the action*] kapow! Splat! Skinned and
gutted and sold as pet food.

### SAYERS

Yeah.

### GARY

Should cut out that top-end mob tomorrow arvo. Are you goin' to put
on a couple of cartons for the boys?

### SAYERS

Don't I always?

### GARY

Yeah, I've gotta say, you do.

### SAYERS

But I've got that reporter and a photographer coming up to interview
me about those circles later in the afternoon, and I don't want any of
the boys sticking their noses in. A bunch of pissed shearers will be
more than those city wimps can handle.

GARY

You keep the beer flowing and we'll keep out of it.

SAYERS

Do you reckon you could give us a hand this weekend and help me
rip those rabbit warrens out from the 20 acres?

GARY

How much?

SAYERS

Fifty bucks.

GARY

A hundred and you've got a deal.

SAYERS

I'll have the ripper on the tractor ready to go –

> its single tine
> inserted like a prick
> in a hole that is entry
> to a rabbit warren
> it moves like a war criminal
> carrying out orders
> with ruthless efficiency –
> pneumatically lowered
> with a hiss from the tractor,
> disembowelling
> the red earth
> with relentless savagery,
> its single fang dripping
> wantonly.

GARY

Okay, make it fifty!

*Laughter. Fade out.*

## Scene 5

*The stage is in darkness except for a light outside the Town Hall.* LEN *and* JO *are standing beneath it.*

JO

So what time did this guy say he'd be here?

LEN

Nine. It's ten past now. Should be any minute.

JO

I'm not thrilled about staying at his place. Let's go to the hotel and charge it.

LEN

Yeah, it's a real shithole – give me the Dubai Hilton any day. Anyway, we'd be staying at "his place" if we went to the hotel; he owns it. In fact he owns most of the town.

JO

He might own what's on the surface but he doesn't own what's underneath.

LEN

Well, he does actually. At least he owns all that's worth having underneath. He extracted the spirit of the place and sold it off long ago. As you'll see tomorrow, the area is ravaged by salinity. He owns the higher ground, the rich soil. They cleared the scrub a hundred years back, and when the trees went, the water table rose – dragging the salt out of the soil to the surface. In some parts it's covered in salt crystals – like hot snow!

JO

The land has its own way of saying things.

LEN

You're not kidding. And it's saying what it said to me years back: you

don't belong here. I just want to do this interview and get out of here
pronto. Gives me the creeps being back after all these years.

JO

Yeah, I was from around here myself – I think. Can't be sure – my
foster parents kept things from me. But here seems a likely place . . .
I'd like to think the land will win out in the end, that its spirit is lying
somewhere deep, beyond people like this Sayers.

LEN

Don't underestimate Sayers! He's persecuted almost everyone in the
district at one time or another. My Uncle has been battling him for
decades. Sayers has got the money and the temperament for long-term
feuds.

JO

Great, just what I need!

LEN

Don't worry, he'll treat us with kid gloves, even if he does work out
Clem's my uncle. If he's contacted the paper, he's got something going
that will mean profit for him.

JO

[Loading her camera with film.] The darkness is close here.

LEN

The problem with these sorts of things is that they get right out of
hand so easily, and we're the ones who help them get out of hand.
[Suddenly.] There's a car. It's probably him. It won't be so bad. He'll shut
us away in some distant wing of his grotesquely large house, and we'll
wake up to a fresh start.

Fade out.

# Act 2

## Scene 1

*The stage setting is the same as in Act One, but instead of the Town Hall there is a raised lookout on high ground separating the vistas. This lookout is mounted from back stage, so that it looks down towards the audience. The whole time the action goes on the* GREENIE *is leaning against a corner post of the lookout, moving to the opposite side to the action, though always facing the action. So when the players are "addressing" the green lands, he's on the side of the salt, and vice versa. It begins with him on the salt side, facing* LEN, JO, *and* SAYERS, *who are looking down at the unseen crop circles in the green field. The stage on the green side is littered with the blue bags of circular hay bales, harvested green for the fodder market – these may be images projected onto the background.*

GREENIE

Hay baled in body bags
chemical blue under the hard blue sky
enzymal to intensify
the growth of pigs in sheds,
to build bodies that will fill the plate.
And gravel pits that lead to markets,
hills red and crumbling with extrusion,
the ochre blood seeping through the skin
ground down to knuckles, balls of feet,
ghost gums clawing at the extremities
of paddocks bulging with caches of enzymes,
the heat at the centre of coiled hay
so intense they might explode
and light the countryside –

a flourish of nutrient
and flesh and debt.

LEN

[*Staring into the distance.*] Well, I've got to say, it's exactly as you described it last night. And you say you came up here on the night of the meteorite, and saw rings of white light glowing in the crop. These rings are the residue, so to speak?

SAYERS

[*Enthusiastically, but with a certain amount of suspicion.*] Saw the whole thing. Drove the Statesman straight up here. It was incredible, like out of this world. Those rings glowing as white as my missus's bum. There aren't really words to describe it . . . as far as I know . . .

LEN

An ontological experience?

[*Pause.*]

SAYERS

I said there were no words to describe it.

LEN

[*Ignoring* SAYERS *and turning to* JO *who has been setting up her camera.*] Get some shots from up here and then we'll go down for some close ups.

SAYERS

No, mate – off limits. Haven't been checked for safety yet.

JO

[*Holding a light meter up.*] There's something wrong with this light.

SAYERS *attempts to look at the meter but* JO *positions herself so that he can't. There is obvious tension between them.*

SAYERS

It's a clear day, what's wrong with it?

JO

[*Half to herself.*]

The sky's too blue,
the light's too harsh.
The colours aren't right.
No matter how narrow
the aperture,
how fast the film,
I just know it's going
to be over-exposed.

SAYERS

[*To* LEN.] What's she on about?

LEN, *taking notes, ignores him.*

JO

[*To* SAYERS.] This was always going to happen. I'm a witness and a
victim. We're all victims – even you, Sayers.

*Fade out.*


## Scene 2

*The salt side of the stage is illuminated.* GREENIE *stands by, watching on.*

WRIGHT

That out of the sand plain
water would run down to the dam
even in summer – in dry

territory the obvious
place to settle. By association

[27]

the house & then the entire
property became known
as Sandsprings. It was rumoured
that its significance

was much greater than local
hearsay, that once whole tribes
moved to & from its sharp

cool waters as the crazy
Gool-boort sang
the banksia blossom.

[*continuing in a distracted voice*]

It's as if the land itself
flows with time.
Constantly changing,

occupying and abandoning itself.
But then, we've altered
its flow, upset the hydraulics.

CINDY

I like to think we'll get it to a state where it can look after itself again.
That's what the town elected me to do, so I'm going to make sure I
come up with the goods.

MARY

It will be hard work – and don't forget he almost had it over you.
[*Almost sadly.*] Would have been nice if a few more votes had gone your
way.

CINDY

You only need one more than the opposition. And anyway, if we
manage the situation in an economically viable way, they'll soon see
the benefits.

MARY

Oh, it worries me hearing words like "economically". That usually means compromise.

CINDY

[*Annoyed, betraying something deeper.*] You've got to be a realist, Mary. I mean, for example, if these crop circles should start generating tourist money, it'll be all to the good. When the coffers are full we can put money into the schools, and help support tree planting. And we might get free advertising from the papers – I was having a word in your nephew's ear today . . .

WRIGHT

[*Suddenly, coming from somewhere else.*] It's bigger than any effort we'll make. The land's got its own inner resilience. The changes wrought now have little meaning in the grand scheme of things.

CINDY

Normally I'd agree with you. But that theory works on the principle that humans won't continue to intervene, and they will.

MARY

As custodians, we are responsible. Unless that custody is taken away from us.

CINDY

Yes.

WRIGHT

[*Lost in thought.*] That's a hundred-and-twenty-thousand trees we've planted, and still the salt grows. Ring after ring surrounding it and still it pushes through, and kills the most salt-resistant strains. A fresh outbreak on the Jacksons' property and we're under threat again. We've all got to work together.

MARY

[*To* CINDY.] It's funny, I often sit in here of an evening and look out over the wastes. When I was young I lived on Hathaways, a property just down the road. It was rich and very English in winter. My mother spoke prayers at the table giving thanks for our good fortune. I spoke with my brother in this room last week and he'd almost forgotten how it was. To him it's just the wreckage after the flood.

I still feel
the jump of the heart
in catching nightlights
on the rise of the paddocks

or on hearing the foxes
barking high up
on the Needlings hills

and I recall our spinster sister
hanging washing with stockings
covering her arms, her pale skin
hidden from the midday sun.

WRIGHT

[*Almost to himself, combative.*] We've got to work together . . .

CINDY

That's the point I've been trying to make – so everyone's interests are served.

*Pause.*

MARY

[*In her own world.*] My brother works as a bank manager in Holding Brook now, with his wife running the small property she inherited from her father. He's not interested in it. She does all the work. She tells people [*mimicking her sister's voice.*]

He's in town, working at the bank,
convenient actually. One of the few
times managers & their clients

get on. I mean, he never really liked
the work though he'd hate to lose
the farm. He loves the birds.

Especially the red-capped parrots
& that tawny frogmouth that's been
up by the top gate for years.

The only joke he ever made was
that I'm in love with John Deere,
my tractor, but what the other

blokes did with that nugget shut
him up real quick. And he doesn't
"excuse" me with "buts", like

"but she has a voice as sweet
as honey" or "but she dresses so
delicately & sews her own clothes".

It's that time of year, the best
time when the rufous hay has been cut
& set in stooks like it should be.

I like the old ways – the same family's
been stooking here as long as any
of my family can remember.

*Fade out.*


## Scene 3

WRIGHT *is showing* LEN *around the property. As we know, they are uncle
and nephew; Len has been away for a long time.*

LEN

So, you sold Grandpa's place?

#### WRIGHT

Had to. It was good land, Len, but we needed the money to work on
saving the bulk of the farm.

> Went back to Dad's place
> last week & the new bloke
> didn't recognize me – thought
> I might be his mail-order partner
> from the city. I told him I'd
> sold him the place, that once,
> as far as the eye could see,
> my family worked the ochre
> earth. But he ignored me,
> kicking at a tuft of smokebush,
> muttering something about
> making a few changes,
> strengthening the fences.

#### LEN

There seems to have been a lot of selling off in recent years. Sayers's
holdings have swollen to obscene proportions, it seems he's bought
most of the good land.

#### WRIGHT

Yeah, he and some speculators from the city, like the one that didn't
recognize me. There are still a few hobby farms down near the river,
but Sayers's been putting the squeeze on them as well.

#### LEN

What do you think of his crop circles, Uncle Clem?

#### WRIGHT

He's up to something. [*And almost incoherently.*] He's messing with a
dangerous thing . . .

#### LEN

[*Reassuringly.*] I'd guess he's trying to rouse up a little business in town.
Tourists to feed his shops. There's not a lot else to attract them up

from the city.

WRIGHT

That's what Cindy reckons.

LEN

Who's Cindy?

WRIGHT

Town doctor – the Mayor.

LEN

Oh, the Mayor . . . Not convinced by what she had to say.

WRIGHT

Look, she's a friend. At any rate, we've got to keep an eye on Sayers.

People will look at photographs
and believe what they see,
but cameras see only what
they are allowed – I mean
take these rings of lush growth
on this salty scab, a few
months back on bare ground
they'd been the resting place
for dead lambs. And now
the grass is thick and high
because the soil
has been nourished
with their deaths . . .

*They are scanning the distance when they spot the* DIVINER. *He enters from the wings on the salt side of the stage. He is carrying a bent piece of wire and walking with a steady step, eyes fixed to the ground.* WRIGHT *greets him but he continues past them before stopping, hesitating then looking up. His look is one of wonder and irritation. Who has disturbed his precious work?*

WRIGHT

G'day. Can I help you?

DIVINER

[Bemused.] Help me?

WRIGHT

This is my land, you're trespassing.

DIVINER

Your land?

WRIGHT

I can see you're divining.

DIVINER

You, help me?

WRIGHT

Are you lost?

DIVINER

[After a long pause.] I'm following the stream. Tracking the flows.

WRIGHT

Well, you'll only find salt down there. And a mess it is. The capillaries are bruised. We ripped the trees out and the water table rose up, bringing the salt with it. We've woken a sleeping giant.

DIVINER

The wire tells me. I only listen to the wire.

LEN

[Fascinated.] I've read about this but I've never seen it. [Pulls out his notepad.]

WRIGHT

Where are you tracking the "flow" from?

DIVINER

The source. It's the circulatory system of the land, the hydraulics which feed and shape the surface.

LEN

I've read it creates an electrical current. A kind of . . .

WRIGHT

[*A little angry.*] Now look, state your business or get on your bike. You're on private property.

DIVINER

No, it's all linked, there are no fences, only blockages, but then the flow finds an alternative path. It is molecular.

WRIGHT

Mumbo jumbo. Sounds like our bloody Minister.

DIVINER

The power in this ground is strong.

WRIGHT

My power.

DIVINER

It's not your power, it's nothing to do with you.

LEN

Waterwitching, it's also called waterwitching.

DIVINER

The flows are forcing out the poison. It will burst out over the ripened surface and consume. But beneath, the hydraulics will be stronger than ever. It's cleaning itself now.

WRIGHT

Sayers sent you!

DIVINER

The wire . . .

LEN

In Victorian England Diviners were . . .

*The* DIVINER *starts to recite, liturgically. The others stare nonplussed, and as he continues his recital the stage bleeds in red light.*

DIVINER

The Dry Multitudes
await the moisture –

the Diviner requests space,
loosening his collar.

Flies sap his strength,
dams of sweat are breached.

For many the hooked wire
refuses to move – for those
with the gift the feeling
is electric – an extension

of the body, a condensing
of Tractability and Energy.

[*Pause.*]

An appetite for revelation –
the Unseen foiling the skeptics.

The wire taking control
and spinning madly, severing

shirt buttons, piercing the palm:
a stigmata of the rough edges.

And should waters erupt
and the course be tracked

the Dry Multitudes will turn
their backs – a trick they'll say,

and drinking deep in the waste's
red light, deny their thirst.

*Fade out.*


## Scene 4


*It's Sunday service. Most of the townfolk are present. But instead of being
held at the church it's on the "ground" below the lookout.*


MINISTER

I've asked you to gather here today as I believe we've been blessed by
God. The visitation on Sayers's property will mean good fortune for
this town.


WRIGHT

A bloody Anglican Minister who's gone evangelical is a dangerous
thing. Last week this guy was the most conservative Minister this side
of Canterbury.


CINDY

They've got a relatively liberal guy in Canterbury now.


WRIGHT

Whatever . . . He's either been touched or money's got the better of
him – Sayers's managed to buy him off. It's the first time I've ever seen
that bastard at a Church service. The first time.


MARY

Next he'll be putting into the collection plate.

Heaven forbid.

*She and* MARY *laugh but* WRIGHT *is agitated and kicking at the ground.*
*Suddenly he hesitates and stares at the ground. In the background the*
MINISTER *is reading the lesson: from the Song of Solomon. Slowly* WRIGHT
*gets to his hands and knees and scoops his hand into the ground. The lights*
*pan away from him, revealing the contents of his hand slowly. The light ends*
*up on* JO *who has her camera facing where the congregation, now entirely*
*shrouded in darkness, is listening to the Song of Solomon.*

JO

In search of subjects for my portfolio
I stop and set up my camera at the juncture
where Station Road crosses
the overflow, where the salty river
vanishes beneath a sandbank
undercutting the taut carcass
of a kangaroo, its tail
rotted hollow. As I work the shutter
the crop circles hum celestially.
I picture the Bible's leather binding –
stretched like the skin of the dead kangaroo –
the stained glass windows shadowing
the mirror and the lens of the camera.
And I visualize The Book of Photography:
"The soft light of an overcast day
intensifies the warm hues."
Checking the light meter
I expose the mental picture
of my earlier subject (the church,
its windows, the cemetery,
the absence of Nyungar graves) –
fixing the reading with memory . . .

*Fade out.*

# Act 3

## Scene 1

*A couple of weeks later. Instead of the lookout, we now have the façade of a farmhouse. This will be alternately the residences of* WRIGHT, SAYERS, *and* LUCY. *The story has broken. Tourists, (the curious, the quacks, and the skeptics) are flooding into town.*

GREENIE

A pair of foxes
lie in death together
untouched by the hunter:
an expression
of devotion –
reductio ad absurdum –
like the poor dog
starving on the grave
of its master – held up
as human virtue
in an animal.
A crop duster crazy
in its dives over the hill
affects longevity,
silently we share
a strange sort of destiny.
A pair of foxes lying
on straw in a deserted pig shed
probably dined
on strychnine – a stimulant,
an analogy for love.

*After the heralding of the* GREENIE *who speaks his lines from the extreme left of the salt side of the stage, the light fills the stage.* WRIGHT *is sitting on a wooden block in front of the salt, looking out onto the audience.*

WRIGHT

Like amateur archaeologists in Arcadia
They come to scour the fields
For extra-terrestial paraphernalia.
Paddocks are plundered
Of skulls and vertebrae,
Plough discs and tines,
A sun blue bottle is worshipped
And the salt gives off rays of longevity.

Everything dead has been touched with mystery. The commonplace is now an item to be treasured. Years of reclamation are being trodden into the dirt.

Blue heron walks on water –
a clear morning, a second front
passing over, the dam red

& swollen, flooded heart
of the varicose paddock.
Blue heron walks on water –

that's what the city folk
think, not knowing there's
a pumping platform

just below the surface.
Blue heron walks on water –
a mid-winter miracle.

[*Continues angrily.*] The town's abandoned its schemes, the land has been lost. A quick buck. They've been caught up in the frenzy. If only we'd managed to keep it out of the papers. It's as if the grain has been infected by ergot and they've all gone mad. Seeing things that aren't there. They're all claiming to see meteorites and strange lights at night. Some of them have even been chased in their cars. Where will it stop? The weather's turning and the harvest's coming. Sparse as the crops are, they will need harvesting. But there is only conflict with the land. Wringing it dry for every phantasmagorical drop.

[*The* DIVINER *comes onto the stage from the green side. He is being pulled around by the wire which is twitching, as if possessed.*]

Hey there fellow, what are you doing back? I thought I sent you packing last time. [*The* DIVINER *persists in his frantic motions.*]

[*Pause.*]

Looks like you've got Saint Vitus' dance, or maybe you've been poisoned like the rest of the town.

DIVINER
[*Suddenly and rapidly.*] The flow has been corrupted. Poison floods the subterranean. Driven to the surface it is deflected back to the source. It is drowning in its own fluid. The waste cannot be flushed to the surface. The surface is sealed. [*He is dragged by the divining rod off stage.*]

WRIGHT
Another one on the scrapheap. Like the district's neglected machinery. But it's not only this crop circle thing, it's been the way since this land was occupied . . . [*He hesitates, picks up a stick, draws circles in the dirt, and then, as if angry with himself*] since it was stolen! It's been invaded and now we don't know what to do with our victory. Pyrrhic victory, this one? Even the harvest, supposedly a time of bounty, is a war against nature. The Header is a war machine moving like death amongst the whispering ears of wheat . . .

Shoes once shod in a blacksmith's shop
rust on hooves lying on the rough edge
        of a paddock, horse skeletons
mingle with broken hoppers & elevators
    & the iron-ringed wheels of surface strippers −

sprouted grain thick on the
ground, like chemically stimulated hair.

The warped screens of a seed cleaner
buried to the knees in clay and salt, snake their
    way up towards the stunted fruit trees'
low slung fruit like apodal spirits in a venomous

light – winter hot on its heels. Inside the shed
    the bellows groan in their frame
of blackbutt & mudbrick, the coal for the fire-

box lies scattered like shoddy talismans,
   & the anvil sits sullenly, a dead lodestone.

CINDY *enters from green side of stage.*

### CINDY

Ah, Clem, Mary said I'd find you sulking down here. She reckons
you've dropped your bundle.

### WRIGHT

[*Eyeing her sceptically.*] Yeah, well, I've spent a lot of years trying to
surround the islands of salt. Circle after circle of trees. [*He continues to
draw circles in the dirt and seemingly loses himself in his task.*]

### CINDY

You shouldn't give in. I've got a feeling that things will turn out all
right. The town's been doing well. We've got extra money in the
coffers. A war chest if you like.

### WRIGHT

[*Disdainfully.*] It'll get so big it'll burst and shower you with shrapnel.

### CINDY

I'll tell you about a little something I watched in the skies over the
Town Hall today, I think it'll appeal to you:

Three New Holland honey-eaters
harassed a young wedge-tailed eagle.

Sweeping and looping and dropping
it shook them off. It persisted in its

original flight. It encroached
on territories as if it owned the place.

The honey-eaters renewed their assault
and the eagle broke away, lost them

and then repeated the act. Again
they attacked until it suddenly

lifted dramatically high, encircled them below,
then vanished into the steely blue.

*Fade out.*


## Scene 2

SAYERS's *place.* SAYERS *and* GARY *are drinking on the verandah. There is
an amber light which makes them slightly difficult to see. Their movements
should cast murky shadows.*

GARY

I wouldn't mind gettin' into her pants.

SAYERS

Yeah, she's a bit of a looker, that dyke bitch.

GARY

Don't know what she sees in that clod hoppin' pig of hers. It looks like
someone's got to her with a handpiece. [*They laugh and drink.*] You
know, I reckon if I could get her on her own, she'd go for me.

SAYERS

[*Laughing so much he coughs up his beer and makes a scene about the mess over his jacket.*] Who, the clod hoppin' pig? Gunna give the pig a good arse fucking, eh?

GARY

Fuck off! [*Play fighting* SAYERS.] You'd better watch it boy or I'll give your rich arse a good kickin'.

[*Pause.*]

Hey, got any good videos inside?

SAYERS

Feel like watching Pulp Fiction again?

GARY

Yeah . . . [*but he's suddenly distracted. A car's pulled onto the house road and he's tracking it with his eyes.*] Looks like you've got visitors.

SAYERS

What's fuckin' unusual. It's probably the missus gettin' back from the city. She's due any day now. Tell you what, if she brings that fuckin' poodle back with her – I warned her! Leave it with your fuckin' sister I said.

[*There's a long pause while they both track the vehicle.*]

Well, it's not her. Looks like the fuckin' Minister's car.

GARY

Yeah, well, you converted him. [*They both laugh and push each other around and start to sing together.*]

The ol' brown bull said lets have anothery
down by the scrubbery
I'll supply the rubbery,
the ol' brown cow said you can go to buggery

I'm not rootin' no more . . .

*The* MINISTER *enters from the salt side of the stage. He's dressed casually, but smartly. He carries a briefcase.*

GARY

Woof, woof . . . hey, where's your collar. Did they let you off for the day? [SAYERS *and* GARY *nearly collapse laughing. The* MINISTER, *obviously flustered, tries to keep a grip on the situation.*]

MINISTER

Sayers . . . hmmm, Gary . . . Sayers, I've got to talk to you about this weekend's service . . . I was hoping to conduct it from actually inside one of the circles.

SAYERS

[*Suddenly sober, sharp-eyed.*] And why would that be?

MINISTER

Well . . . it would be . . . well, more spiritual . . .

SAYERS

I've told you before, no one's to go near the circles. You can have your service on the viewing platform. I'll even arrange catering. [*He laughs.*]

MINISTER

[*A dark look flooding his face.*] People are starting to talk about your unwillingness to allow people close to the circles . . .

SAYERS

What are you implying?

MINISTER

[*Cagily.*] Nothing, really . . . Wright's been making a stink . . .

GARY

He'd better shut it or he might find a dead kangaroo in his bed . . . [*He and* SAYERS *turn to each other, point and say together . . .* ] The Godfather

[45]

... Australian style.... [*Laughter.*]

MINISTER
[*Flustered.*] Well then, on the platform ...

SAYERS
I'm not so sure now ... What do you reckon, Gary?

GARY
For a fee ...

SAYERS
Yeah, five bucks a head ... you round the flock up and we'll charge the
slaughtering price.

MINISTER
[*Disgusted.*] I'll ring you tomorrow ...

SAYERS
Yeah, yeah, you do that ...

*The* MINISTER *leaves.*

GARY
Those scientists will be up tomorrow.

SAYERS
Well, it's my property and they can bugger off.

*Fade out.*

## Scene 3

*Only the green side of the stage is lit,* SAYERS's *house in the centre background. Right front stage,* JO *is photographing the rings with a tripod-
mounted camera. It is hard to discern, but on* SAYERS's *verandah,* GARY *is
cleaning his rifle.* LEN *enters from the left, appearing out of the dark.*

LEN

*[Moves over next to* JO, *and points into the distance.]* On that rise you might be able to just make out what they call the Devil's Backbone around here. There's a native title claim on it at the moment, but it hasn't got much of a chance; Sayers is pouring everything he can into defending it. It's on his land. Recently the rocks have been vandalized. But from a distance, they're still incredibly majestic.

JO

Majestic? Strange word to use. But then, like the name you've given it, Devil's Backbone, it's just another example of cultural imperialism.

LEN

I'd agree, and I'm sorry to say I don't know the traditional name. But ignorance doesn't mean I'm not concerned – I describe it out of the culture I'm most familiar with.

Arched backbone – high above the core –
curves, infiltrates, cools, and sets

rapidly as the surface retreats, as the forest
lifts and the sky, a sheet of dry ice, slips

from season to season, beating a hasty
retreat like defeated mirages, quenching

light and knuckling down, dismantling the crust
of the Devil's Dante-esque flesh –

the flesh all fire and breath dry.
The backbone rests despite its bed shifting

under the plains of Heaven, singing whiplash
against the painted rocks.

JO *continues to take photos while* LEN *muses.*

[47]

## JO

[*Suddenly.*] I never knew my parents but my mother was from the Nyungar people and this is Nyungar land. That's why I asked for the job. I don't really have much of a connection with my people. But I want to find out . . .

[*Pause.*]

I was re-colonized.

*Fade out.*

## Scene 4

LUCY's *place. The façade is lit but the light crosses over into both the green and the white areas of the stage.* LUCY *is spinning yarn and singing.*

### LUCY

O the winter it is past
And the summer's come at last
And the birds they are singing in the trees
Their little hearts are glad
But mine is very sad
For my true love is far away from me.

*She continues to spin yarn, humming the tune. Enter* GARY *carrying his rifle and a dead rabbit. He stands a short way from her. She looks up, continues to spin, and hum. There is a painful lapse of time before he throws the rabbit at her feet.*

### GARY

[*Slightly embarrassed.*] Brought you that. It's fresh, shot this morning.

[*Pause.*]

I'll skin it if you want.

LUCY

[*Stopping and staring at him, with a slightly disgusted expression on her face but managing to keep it under control.*] Well, you know I don't eat meat . . . [*she then says quickly*] . . . but I've got friends that do, so thanks.

*Pause.*

GARY

Why don't you eat . . . ? [*He lets the question wander off and starts tracing circles in the dirt with his boot*]. You know, I'm sorry about giving you a hard time out at the lookout that time your . . . girlfriend . . . was up here. I was pissed. In fact I've been pissed for a couple of months . . . well, I'm not pissed now . . . I get full of myself and become a real prick . . . but I pay for it, I'm paying for it now . . . but you know, I'd never seen a girl kissing a girl before.

*Pause.*

LUCY

How are you paying for it?

GARY

Conscience, I suppose. It's bad when you can't tell anyone . . .

LUCY

Why can't you?

GARY

I'm not sure really.

[*Pause.*]

It's not long till harvest. The crops are starting to turn . . .

LUCY

Yeah, not that we've got much to worry about here. Only half the place is fit for cropping. We're on the border I guess between the salt and the immaculate lands of Sayers.

[49]

GARY

I wouldn't be so sure that they're immaculate ...

LUCY

What do you mean?

GARY

Ah, nothing really ... [*he stops tracing circles with his boot, places the rifle up against the verandah post, and moves close to* LUCY.] I didn't think dykes spun yarn and did things like that ...

LUCY

[*Amused, but uncomfortable with his closeness.*] And do dishes, and cook, and drive tractors, and watch television. [*She laughs but catches it with a closed hand.*]

GARY

[*Slightly prickly.*] Give us a break, you know what I mean.

LUCY

Well, not really ...

*Pause.*

GARY

[*Leaning over her, examining the yarn.*] Well, it's a good job you're doing ...

LUCY

[*Moving away.*] Phew, a little breathing space.

GARY

[*Sharply, aggressively – offended.*] Well, fuck you madam.

LUCY

[*Quickly.*] Hey, come on, loosen up – I get phobic being in crowds.

GARY

[*Who has moved back and is picking up his rifle.*] I'd better go now. Enjoy the rabbit – well, anyway, hope your girlfriend enjoys the rabbit.

LUCY

Thanks.

[*Pause* – GARY *lingers*, LUCY *averts her eyes, toys with the yarn.*]

Listen Gary, you're an all right kind of bloke when you're sober; don't worry about me, I've got attitude. You get like that. It's not easy having to put up with you and your gang.

[*She starts to laugh and despite himself* GARY *does as well. There is a genuine moment of collusion between them. They look each other straight in the eye.*]

But I tell you something Gary, Sayers is a worry, he's dangerous. There's something dark in him. He undresses women with his eyes. I know he's your mate but I'd watch him. He'll stab you in the back.

GARY

[*Male pride aroused.*] I'll be fucked he will. He just pays for the piss. I don't owe him anything. I see things, don't you worry. But I use him, not the other way around. And I know one or two things that'd fry him if they got out.

LUCY

Well boy, you just watch out for him, if you've got anything over him that'll make him even more of a problem.

GARY

Don't you worry about me, but watch your own arse. He's after it.

LUCY

I know.

GARY

[*Awkwardly.*] Well, I'm off . . .

LUCY *watches* GARY *go. Shakes her head in disbelief, and slowly resumes* *spinning and humming. The scene fades out with her singing again. The* DIVINER *is seen dimly in the background.*

LUCY

[*Sings.*]
    O the winter it is past
    And the summer's come at last
    And the birds they are singing in the trees
    Their little hearts are glad
    But mine is very sad
    For my true love is far away from me.

*Fade out.*

## Scene 5

*The* MINISTER *is standing on his own in front of the salt, spotlighted. He is* *dressed in full garb, with a book in hand. If possible, a dry wind should be* *disturbing his garments, blowing across the stage towards the green side.* *The lighting should be blood red, deep blues, interchanging to give an* *Apocalyptic effect.*

MINISTER

And should faith collect
    in spiralled stalks
of hay.

And should faith lodge
    in the stressed metal
of machinery

And should faith rest
    in the gaps between stones
of a well

And should faith lay aside
    fatigue in a bellow-driven
forge

And should faith watch
    from the wings of a shearing
shed

And should faith hang at our heels,
    a stray wind – harsh,
persistent.

*Fade out – sound of wind reaches crescendo and as it fades we hear the* MINISTER *reading from Revelation – "I am the Alpha and the Omega". This persists for about thirty or forty seconds before silence.*

# Act 4

## Scene 1

*Harvest time. The green fields are now yellow. Large rectangular hay bales*
*decorate the horizon. The façade is once again the Town Hall.*

GREENIE

Harvest time. Green fields
are now yellow,
most are still bare.
Some grow whiter,
the salt spreading further.
Hay bales like stele or crypts
or the residue of sun
in a sea of Horus's wheat
like stone ships friezing
sun-driven hydraulics,
the Green River running
darkly through the valley.
Totemic and primal they
lean into their shadows,
the blond floor of harvest
listless at their bases: these uprights
of antipodean stonehenges
temporal and mocking
the chthonic source of their
construction, commodities
that might explode with heat.
Cyclical and ephemeral
the hawk that dives for skinks,
and the cockatoos

perched like gargoyles –
eyes twisted to leers in masks.
The pattern of the machine
as it configures the paddock,
space contradicting
the brief time they persist sub-
consciously, rolling there
like chaotic empires
nearing the end of their days,
their situations as delicate
as the southern forest's
burnt orange haze, burnback
darkening catastrophe's fuel
like a dare, while nearby
stookers build ricks –
small offerings in fields
of obelisks gloating under
skies known for lightning,
the arsonist's glint.

*Fade out.*


## Scene 2


*Salt side of stage.* WRIGHT *is engaged in the Sisyphean task of transferring water from a bucket with a tiny cup into a sheep water trough. Mary is planting trees.*


WRIGHT

Someone's got to keep the sheep watered. Sayers's harvest is almost in. But everyone else's is spilling to the ground. Too busy with entertaining tourists, or waiting for circles to appear. If a bloody fireball did crash into their paddocks the whole lot'd go up in flames. It's like they've lost all ability to reason. There has been a visitation, and its name is Madness. And they say when I argue the point that the yields are so low it's not worth spending the money to bring it in. That rust has got into the grain anyway, that they won't let it into the bins but send it straight to the feed stack. Rust:

> Occupies and dissolves
> the seams of rainwater tanks,
> riding the galvanized waves
> and leaching down into the soil,
> wheat stalk on wheat stalk,
> spider-fanged scarifier
> on spider-fanged scarifier,
> disc plough on disc plough,
> tractor on tractor,
> flaking bark of salmon
> and white gum.

### MARY

But we must keep going. We can't let it beat us – without us there'd be no one to plant the trees, to stop the rot . . . to slow it down . . .

### WRIGHT

[*Hasn't heard her.*]
> the emphatic rust
> seeding both sides of the fenceline,
> rufous brown,
> blood-brown.
> The sun playing tricks
> giving it life.

Yesterday I wandered down to the South Paddock to spend time at my father's, my mother's, my grandfather's grave . . .

> it's weird visiting the grave –
> three boxes of ashes piled in a hole
> & covered with blue metal
> in the corner of the meshed
> enclosure – rusty traps
> hang on the fence,
> steel jaws as indifferent

[56]

as sheep bones strewn
about the paddocks.

MARY

sheep nibbling the turf about
the house-garden's edge,
the house a headstone,
the plover edgy
as a spotter plane flies overhead
as all are lulled
into a long summer sleep

WRIGHT

I've not seen the Diviner since the day he went crazy. Somehow I feel
a need for him to appear. To track the flow of clean water. To map out
the channels of poison. But he won't, I sent him packing. And that was
a long time ago . . .

*Fade out.*

## Scene 3

CINDY *and* LEN *are standing outside the Town Hall.* JO *is taking photo-graphs.*

LEN

It seems pretty odd that you had plenty to say against Sayers last time
we spoke and now you almost seem to be defending him.

CINDY

I'm not defending him, I'm representing the Town. I'm responsible
not only for their physical health but also for their general well-being.
For the first time in years the townsfolk are optimistic. People are
coming to Green Springs. Sayers has put it back on the map.

LEN

A little bit pastoral isn't it?

CINDY

If you want to put it that way. All of this seems strange coming from you – I got the impression you couldn't stand being back here. Didn't think we'd see you again.

LEN

Well, in some sense I feel responsible for the disease that's infected this town, and I intend to find an antidote.

CINDY

I think you're a little overzealous. And you're no Doctor. Diseases are more in my area.

LEN

Making them or curing them?

CINDY

It strikes me that you're only interested in selling papers.

LEN

No, that's what I was doing before, by proxy anyway. What I should be doing is writing a story on the salt problem . . . You know, my Uncle Clem's spoken highly of you, but thinks you've been hoodwinked by Sayers.

CINDY

Nice man, a friend, but a dreamer. Sadly deluded. Even his wife has lost patience with him. Talk to her, she's got a head on her shoulders.

LEN

With all respect to my Aunty, she's given in. She doesn't believe this rubbish any more than him. She's just concerned for his health.

CINDY

His health? I've never met a more robust man for his age. Physically he's in peak condition. It's only his mind that's at risk.

                              LEN
[*Disgusted.*]
    The vision splendid beyond the last stands of forest,
    looking down from behind Sayers's well-strained fence,
    a brilliant morning, just as it should be,
    farmland sculptured for a landscape artist.
    That double-gees creep up through the undergrowth
    is ignored as long as the salt stays on its side of the fence
    the For Sale signs and closures are kept out of the picture.

                             CINDY
[*Almost laughing.*] You're starting to sound a bit like your Uncle Clem.
I'll leave you people to yourselves now – I've got a lot of work to do.

LUCY *enters as* CINDY *exits.*

                              LUCY
I'm not sure about her.

                              LEN
I know what you mean, but then, I'm not sure about much around
here.

                              LUCY
Well, I'll tell you something, you know Gary – "Gazzer", as they call
him –

                              LEN
I've met him with Sayers. Redneck par excellence.

                              LUCY
Yeah, but that's all bluff – he's an actor constantly in search of an
audience. He actually loathes Sayers. Gary's an opportunist and up
until now thinks he's been having the better of Sayers . . .

LEN

Up until now?

LUCY

Let's just say the seeds of doubt have been sown in his mind. He's starting to click that it's Sayers who's been using him as a kind of stand-over-merchant. Hired muscle. I ran into him in the street a few days ago and he told me Sayers has been calling him Vince.

LEN

Vince?

LUCY

Yeah, as in Vincent Vega from Pulp Fiction.

JO

[*Suddenly taking an interest.*] And you know what happens to Vince.

LEN

It strikes me as more than a little odd that Gary's talking to you, of all people, if you'll excuse my presumption.

LUCY

Yeah, me too. I tell you what − it's been getting pretty scary out at my place. I'm on my own during the week because my girlfriend works in the city and only gets up during the weekends. She's been at me, wants us to leave. She never liked the idea of my moving up here. She calls it redneck country and she's right. And she has a hatred of Gary that knows no bounds. She reckons he'll be around with a gun one night. I think Gary's got problems, but somehow I trust him. He's motivated by pride and testosterone, and if you keep that in mind you can control him. My girlfriend has never forgotten his barking at her, but I tell her that it's in fact Gary that's the dog, actually more of a puppy when you think about it. He came out a while back with a dead rabbit.

JO

A dead rabbit?

                              LUCY

A peace offering . . .

                               JO

Or a warning . . .

                              LUCY

A bit of both I suppose, but the warning's purely subliminal. I think
he needed to confide in someone.

                              LEN

And he confided in you?

                              LUCY

No, not exactly, but he hinted.

                              LEN

How?

                              LUCY

Well, apart from saying he knew things about Sayers that would cause
the bastard trouble, he drew pictures.

                              LEN

Pictures?

                              LUCY

Well, a sand sketch really. A dirt map. I'm not even sure if he did it
consciously, but when he'd left I noticed he'd been scratching in the
dirt. There was a box with three circles in the middle of it.

                              LEN

Sayers's crop circles!

                              LUCY

For sure. I mean, Gary's been spending most of his time drinking and
looking after them. He's a shearer by trade but has scarcely been seen

at work. Too busy looking after Sayers's magic circles. The source of his new-found power.

### LEN

As Uncle Clem says, possessing the townsfolk with the Madness. Poisoning their waters. Speaking of the circles, Uncle Clem sits for hours on end drawing the bloody things. He knows that these circles are a hoax. I think most of the town know it's a hoax but want it to be true. Very few are interested in scrutinizing the things.

### LUCY

Well, Sayers was putting heavy pressure on me to sell up. Our property sits on the border between the salt country and the good soils of his place. He wants to buy us out as a buffer. He's paranoid about the salt.

### LEN

Well, he should plant circles of trees instead of carving crop circles in the middle of his bloody paddocks. Uncle Clem told me an anecdote about lightning striking marri and jarrah trees that somehow seems relevant – not that there are many of either still standing in these parts. The point was, that Sayers's bloody fireball will probably end up consuming him. The sad thing is, you feel that when all this passes, the town will return to its old half-hearted ways, and gradually corrode away into the salt.

Uncle Clem reckons quite a few
of the trees struck in forest
country around these parts
are marri & that when they
are struck an explosion
follows, blowing large
splinters of wood in all
directions. He says
no one is really sure
why this happens
but that it might
have something to do
with the water-filled tree cells

expanding rapidly!
On those occasions
when jarrah is struck
it tends to lose a strip of timber
from strike point to ground.
Sometimes surrounding trees
will die but only those nearby.

*Fade out.*

## Scene 4

*The centre of the stage is blacked out.* WRIGHT *wanders from his spread through to* SAYERS*'s. He is holding a divining rod and is dishevelled.*

WRIGHT
I must find the source, the source of the poison. The wire won't twitch
in my hands. Everything below the salt is dead.

Termites vein deadwood – tattoowork
some have called it. A sheep skull shattered
& sculpted into the shape of a parrot
crashed or brought down suddenly.

A plume of orange fungus gives a dead
stump a taste of the ludicrous, looking
almost vivacious in the strobe light,
plumped against the salty tesserae.

They search for something. A teapot
rust-blue & pocked with a tight grouping
of bullet holes. One of them can even
guess the calibre – triple two. Another
discovers the sound a southerly
makes as it rips through the branches
high overhead. The shed skin of a dugite
is found caught in a fork of deadwood

close to the ground, & they check
to see if the owner hasn't returned.
Empty cartridge cases lie like hollow
notions as the conversation idles
like a kerosene tractor – just brass
pressings & not icons or talismans
worth preserving as memories,
as tools to shape the narrative
when back inside they drink
beer & watch t.v.

[*He wanders into darkness and after a while reappears on* SAYERS*'s land.
The* DIVINER *is shadowing him. Suddenly the wire goes crazy in his hands,
which start to bleed at the palms. He continues until he reaches the crop
circles. A jacket and a gun are lying on the ground. He examines them and
looks around. Crouching down, he scratches at them.*]

That's what he's hiding! A twofold deception! A double vision of
disaster. The corruption can't be held in any longer – the disease is
breaking out.

The alluvial sky
where the blue is so deep
it threatens
even the salt,
the world upside down –
absorbing the clean blood
of the land as these gulleys
with their brackish
puddles fonts
invite the Condemned to wash . . .
the perishing stock
that litters the district,
the crops fallen
to an unseen plague
of locusts, a silent machine
perpetually scissoring
the outline of shadows

cast by the clouds of fancy
over the vast plains . . .

SAYERS *appears at a run, struggling to do up his jacket zip.*

SAYERS
Get off my land, you old bastard! What are you doing here? Fuckin'
divining! Well, you're on private property and I oughta shoot you like
a dog!

WRIGHT
[*Dropping the wire and staring at* SAYERS.] It's been you all along – devil!

SAYERS
What are you on about, you old bastard? [SAYERS *points the gun at*
WRIGHT *and nudges him with the barrel.* WRIGHT *stumbles off, laughing,
the* DIVINER *following. As the scene fades out we hear* WRIGHT *laughing
long and loud.*]

*Fade out.*

## Scene 5

CINDY, MINISTER, MARY *and* SAYERS, *on his land.*

MINISTER
The fig tree withers and will never bear fruit again.

SAYERS
If you don't keep that crazy old bastard off my property I'll shoot him.

CINDY
That won't be necessary. He's just unwell – mentally. Stress.

SAYERS
I don't given a rat's arse what it is – a man's property is sacred. Tell
them that, Minister!

It is true. A man's house is his castle . . . [*continues babbling platitudes.*]

MARY

O shut your face, you sanctimonious fool.

MINISTER

Excuse me, madam, I . . .

CINDY

Now, now – we'll sort this out. I'll prescribe something for stress, it'll settle him down. And if there's further trouble we'll calm him down.

MARY

[*Indignant.*] He's not a dog. And he was your friend, which was more than you deserved.

CINDY

Come on Mary, it's a difficult time for you.

SAYERS

I mean it – if I see him again, I'll shoot the bastard.

MARY

I'd watch it with those threats, Mr Sayers.

CINDY

Come on, Mary, it's not as bad as that.

SAYERS

[*To* MARY.] No one will listen to you. You're a loser, like your old man.

MARY

[*Shaking.*] Judge and ye'll be judged. [*Gradual fade out with spotlight on* MARY, *whose voice dwindles as the following piece is spoken.*]

In deadwood
or on ropes of haze,

suspended
in brittle air
the parrots shimmer
brightly –
　　they hear
your determined steps
across the vacant
paddocks,
　　the crunch of salt
below your boots.

I place my hands
to the surface
of ouija night
& write landfill
& title deeds
like premonitions
across the deck
of wet hessian
that covers
the silo's bare floor.
Without map
or advice
I set out with you
across the salt,
never doubting
the accuracy of your step,
the rites
of harvest.

*Fade out.*

# Act 5

## Scene 1

*It's night and* WRIGHT *is at the crop circles with a polythene sack and a shovel. He is working by gas lantern, digging at the crop circles. The moon is full overhead, but blood red.*

WRIGHT
[*With the exertion that comes with digging.*] You must celebrate, you have to commemorate amnesia, savagery, even the stupidity . . .

[*He shovels dirt into the sack and breaks into a mutter, quoting from Revelation and Isaiah: deserts and Apocalypse. Finishing his work, he sits next to the sack and starts chanting the following lines. He stares at the sky, the ground, into the darkness.*]

Emending context flashfloods of poison
stipulating death as endgame
field mice washed-out & riding
the cracker-barrel towards
a fossil fame

an oily residue emerging
from the paddocks of the richer side
patronizing rainbows
as if they were genuine
offerings

the freaky crosswind
exploits the the silence
of the snake

foul-mouthed & abusive
with the rising water-table,
cutting up the profit
& the usury,
all this atrocity
where the knowing roots
of salmon gums
once drank deep

[*Pause.*]

[*Shrieking.*] It's salt! It's bloody salt blistering up out of the poisoned channels.

SAYERS *appears with his gun.*

SAYERS
[*Beside himself.*] I warned you, you stupid old bastard. Now I'm goin' to shoot you and bury you!

WRIGHT
It's the poison, the poison. It's the source. It flows down into the surrounding lands and poisons them. The salt is not threatening Sayers's lands, it comes from them.

SAYERS *shoots him in the face. Light changes.* GARY *runs onstage.*

GARY
You fucking idiot! You fucking idiot!

SAYERS
I told you if any bastard crossed me they'd have to deal with the consequences, with the "Great Vengeance and Furious Anger"! I didn't get this far for nothing. This is my town, and no bastard's going to trespass.

[GARY *is staring blankly at the body of* WRIGHT.]

Now fuckin' help me dump him on the back of the ute and we'll grind him up for the pigs.

[GARY *continues to stare.*]

Come on you slimy bastard, or I'll put a bullet in you as well.

*With this,* GARY *lunges at* SAYERS. *There is a fierce struggle and* GARY *is shot in the ankle. But he manages to get* SAYERS *in a head-lock and disarm him.*

GARY

Now listen to me, if you so much as twitch I'll break your fucking neck. You're an evil bastard. It's as if everything that's bad in the world is running through your veins. Wright was worth a hundred of you. Twenty years older and he still could have flogged you if he'd wanted to. Using a gun – you gutless prick. All your bullshit, all your plots and plans and working things out to the final detail, all end in one thing – fucking violence. I should stick that fucking gun up your arse.

*With this* SAYERS *begins to struggle again.* GARY *strengthens his hold.*

I'm warning you you bastard! I'm fucking warning you!

*Blackout.*

## Scene 2

*Outside the church. A funeral service. The whole town is there. The entire backdrop is white.* MARY *speaks to the congregation. The* MINISTER *and* CINDY *keep their heads bowed during the entire scene.*

MARY

I have come to you
when the moon has been dead,
and sought illumination
and thought – the foolish fire

transforming deserts into forests
into rivers, and these Jack-O-Lanterns
making sense of it all,
always vigilant,
always with me.
Late light and waterbirds
are incoming over the tawny fields,
settling on the summer-low
rungs of the dams, the frosted
surface of the salt pans,
the black banks
of the sluggish river.
That in this dry place
the waterbirds come,
including that elusive night heron
with the weight of the old world
on its shoulders, hidden
during the sharp light of day,
patrolling the shallows
between sunset and sunrise,
like a visitation
in a twilit world
where animal and human
cohabit, where souls are . . .

*She steps aside, comforted by* LEN *and* LUCY. *There is a long silence while The Order For The Burial of The Dead is read. This is followed by the entry from the left side of the stage of the* DIVINER *who is garbed in a suit and carrying a briefcase with his divining rod sticking out of a pocket.*

DIVINER
Here is to be noted, that the Office ensuing is not to be used for
    any
that die unbaptized, or excommunicate, or have laid violent
    hands upon themselves.
Vandals disguised as priests have broken angels; we attempt to
    rebuild them but settle on laying

their body parts in what we assume to be the right positions – a
wing
grounded like a Senegal dove or parrot struck by a car
thundering through the country.

[*Pause.*]

[*In a measured voice.*] Today I came across the carcass of a ram that had
sunk into the salt pan. It smelt as if it had been dead for at least a
week. Normally I'd have walked around it, picking up my trail at a safe
distance on the other side. But the wire wouldn't let me away from
it. It was as if the source lay not underneath the carcass but within. I
drew closer and the wire buzzed, almost red hot. And then I noticed
that what I'd at first taken to be the usual swarm of flies was in fact a
swarm of bees. The bees had hived inside the carcass. The flow was
honey. The dead flesh of the beast was generating bees, restoring the
flow, cleansing the channels that feed the surface. The carcass was the
gateway to the world that had been closed off to us.

*Fade out.*


### Scene 3

*The entire backdrop is green now.* MARY *and* LEN *are on* LUCY's *property,
talking with* LUCY, *and planting trees. They are laughing and generally
happy. The* GREENIE *is standing off to the left.*

GREENIE
Down off the shoulder of the pink granite scarp
down in the rich soil where the stalks are deep,
they replant trees where Sayers had once
cut out circles with lengths of string,
in archetypal patterns that kept us wondering . . .

JO
[*Enters, taking photos as they plant.*] Went out to Devil's Rock this morning, just as the sun was breaking over it. And can you believe it – I

didn't even take a photograph. Tomorrow a couple of mates from Narrogin are heading out to see if they can track down some of the people whose families lived here before the whites. I'll find out the Nyungar name for it yet. Hey Len, you goin' to write a story on the real Devil's Rock?

LEN

No, I'm going to hang around here and plant a few trees. I reckon I've written my last story for a while.

*They laugh. Pause.*

JO

Hey Lucy, I hear you visited Gary today in hospital?

LUCY

Yeah, the infection's down. He'll be out soon.

JO

Sounds like prison . . . appropriate.

LUCY

Well, to a strapping lad like that it is. But it has its rewards – Cindy was paying him special attention . . . [*They laugh again.*]

*There is a long pause during which* JO *swings her camera and starts taking pictures of them and then of the audience.*

JO

[*Still snapping photos.*] Given the right light the camera doesn't lie . . .

*Laughter.* LEN *and* MARY *exit together.*

*Fade out. A short delay before the light returns with only the* GREENIE *on the stage.*

That beneath the rusting
corrugated sheeting
the water is breathing

for the poison and salt
are yearly diminishing . . .
the crop circles

are flourishing –
discs of grain
ringed by trees.

*Fade out.*

THE END

# Smith Street

By John Kinsella and Tracy Ryan with additional
material by Steve Chinna

A melodrama in three acts (or, Sunset Clause)
or
Smith Street (Between Heaven and Hell)

Smith Street was first performed by Theatre Studies students at the
Dolphin Theatre, the University of Western Australia, on 24 May, 2001
with the following cast.

| | |
|---|---|
| ANGEL | Romy Kennedy |
| JACK | Justin Barrett |
| NARRATOR | Jenn Piper |
| MRS WALPURGIS | Annwen Griffiths |
| MR CLIPBOARD | Andrew Hunter-Christy |
| MAGISTRATE | Renita Almeida |
| CLIENT | Sharyl Sapari |
| COP 1 | Kris Bowtell |
| COP 2 | Emma Nicoletti |
| STREET PEOPLE et al | Sharon Davis |
| | Sara Fonck |
| | Tammy Mulder |
| | Yajna Ramasary |

Directed by Steve Chinna.
Stage management by Peter Evans.
Lighting design by Aja Styles.
Music devised and performed by Kris Bowtell and Emma Nicoletti.
Production duties shared by Clarabelle Chaw, Clara Fletcher, and Monique Rampono.
Photographs by Malcolm Crisp.

## Characters

ANGEL, *a young prostitute*
JACK, *her pimp*
NARRATOR, *a butch dyke*
MRS WALPURGIS, *a resident*
MR CLIPBOARD, *a resident*
MAGISTRATE
CLIENT
COP 1
COP 2
STREET PEOPLE, PROSTITUTES, TOURISTS,
RESIDENTS, PARLIAMENTARY
DELEGATION, *etc.*

## The set

*Should be in some way arranged into three distinct sections: Hell, Earth and Heaven. Smith Street winds through all three zones so that the characters can move back and forth between them. There is a conspicuous belltower. There is a peepshow which may simply be depicted by a banner bearing that name, possibly with a rainbow flag. There are blocks of flats, anonymous-looking, as well as a "Tuscan Splendour" in which MRS WALPURGIS lives. We can see into this house. There is a courtroom and the dilapidated interior of a squat.*

# Act 1

## Scene 1

*The street.* CLIENT *is "asleep" on stage – under the Belltower.* TOURISTS
*enter to music.*

TOUR LEADER
Welcome all to Smith Street
Named after a famous thief
A picturesque burlesque
A risqué place of mischief.

Now, stick together, please
don't be wandering off
the denizens are dangerous
they're full of rancorous wrath.
And that's the folk that live here –
the citizens on the hill
Don't worry about the street folk
they can't hate enough to kill.

Here we have a monument
a monumental monument
can anybody tell me
who's responsible for building this?

CLIENT
A priapic pile of phallic pride
a memorial to those who've died
an excremental pile of crap
a symbol of great hubris.

TOURISTS *and* CLIENT *freeze. All others enter running and take up posi-*
*tions. They freeze and then move slowly like automatons.* NARRATOR *enters.*
MR CLIPBOARD *traverses stage during the following.*

NARRATOR
Dawn birds taken for police radio
outside her window
skin no longer a delimiter
they tread their beat in her
dreams
and in the real
Mr Clipboard does his rounds
old man chafes at his sagging pants

not even shopping or baggage
deflects them
we all look the same in the dark

they are two sides of the one appetite
circlingclosing
as small boys
do wheelies

"you waiting for a lift miss?
just checking"

Smith Street: John Citizen, Jane Citizen
and every in-between citizen
everyman, everywoman,
any woman.

ALL *exit, except* ANGEL *and* NARRATOR.

NARRATOR
Starting early today, Angel?

ANGEL
You gotta get them before work.

Lowers the tension levels for the day.

I've always meant to ask you
where you come from.
You just seemed to appear
a few months back out of nowhere.

Where do I come from? Who am I? Why am I here?
A girl from the wrong side of the tracks?
A farm girl lost in the city?
An opportunist from St Kilda or the Cross?
Who knows? What does it matter?
I'm here and the birds are singing in Smith Street
and the cops don't come out this early.

Not what I've heard.

They're only barricading in the evenings.
But I guess it won't be long.

I'm off to get some coffee.
Catch you round.

Yeah, later.

ANGEL *wanders back and forth between hell and heaven, as if waiting for something. After a couple of turns, she leans up against the Belltower and begins to chant the following lines.*

Though so many people live on this street
it is rich in trees, grass, and birds;

there is always a light shining through the night
in the window of a flat – somewhere someone is awake.
You are never alone, it's good to feel safe.
Early morning movers come past throwing papers,
making deliveries of legal and illicit substances.
All cast an eye over me, some checking me out.
I've blown men from all walks of life.
Each has a technique they think especially cool.

NARRATOR

Tell me about it!

ANGEL

Sidling up and taking control
or standing cow-eyed
to draw me to their side.
Then there are the crawlers, who pull you into their car
before you've a chance to suss them out.
One guy moved so fast he had me in there
before I could shout,
almost strangled me except I finally got out.
That's when I took up Jack's offer
to keep an eye on me
though he takes half the earnings
and charges me double for powder.
Here he comes with that sarcastic leer
wondering if there's any action.

JACK *enters.*

JACK

[*Sung.*] I'm the noted name in the robber's game
I shoot my mouth I take no blame
I scream my pride my mouth struck wide
I stream the street I ply my trade
I sell your meat I deal high grade
I cut the stash I hawk your gash
I split the deal the punters squeal

I strut your stuff I call their bluff
I fight to show my bluff's not blow
I strip the park I haunt the dark
I split their heads I wear cut threads
I'm the monster mobster macho man
the street's my gift the sky's my span
I lunch at dusk I spit the husk
to livid spies behind privet eyes
my name is Jack my name is Jack

I spin the name of the oldest game
I give a flick don't give a fuck
you turn a trick hand, hole, or suck
I hold the bag you make a grab
you're spellbound by my gift of gab.

[*Spoken.*]

How's it going, Angel? Got some good gear
coming in this evening, so look sharp.
I like the morning when the air's clean.
Though a bit of carbon monoxide
goes with the territory! Look,
we gotta watch out today,
you know there's been some grumbling
in the community,
the Residents of the Precinct.
They want your sort out of here.
There's a lynch mob forming.
I've heard a whisper from my contact
that the wagons'll be pulling anyone
working this street today. So if you see them,
just keep walking,
and turn into the Trinity
where they can't touch you, okay?

ANGEL

Okay.

JACK

Whatever you do, don't carry any gear.
I won't be far away, but I can't help you
with the cops. And we can't afford hassles,
'cause you still owe me for that last batch.
Even if they lock you up,
I'll get it out of you.

ANGEL

I couldn't give a fuck.

JACK

Oh, you will, bitch.
You don't mess with me.
you know that.

[ANGEL *exits.*]

I've seen some weird shit
over the years – people
melt into pools on the floor,
and then people forgetting
they ever were. You know,
not even obituaries.
I've seen the bad air
come out of the neat
gardens and swallow houses.
I've seen trees transform
into people darker
than the night, sucking
everything in like gravity.

[*Sung.*] The sky turns green the nightbirds scream
it tears my brain shatters the pane
gives my pain an altered frame
my name is Jack my name is Jack
my name is Jack and I'll be back

JACK *exits. Light onto* MRS WALPURGIS *and* MR CLIPBOARD.


                    MRS WALPURGIS
[*Sung.*] There's a body inside this shell
A heart beats behind the armour
Flesh moves beneath the crust
The carapace that shields my ardour

                    MR CLIPBOARD
Not my fault

                    MRS WALPURGIS
Crusts cut off

                    MR CLIPBOARD
Not my fault

                    MRS WALPURGIS
Ironed pleats

                    MR CLIPBOARD
Not my fault

                    MRS WALPURGIS
Best-dressed girl

                    MR CLIPBOARD
Not my fault

                    MRS WALPURGIS
Polished feet!

I had a friend . . . did she know me?
She dressed so strange; what could she show me!

STREETPEOPLE *enter.*

### STREETPEOPLE

Not my fault

### MRS WALPURGIS

Pull the shutters down

### STREETPEOPLE

Not my fault

### MRS WALPURGIS

Support a closing down

### STREETPEOPLE

Not my fault

### MRS WALPURGIS

Drive them off the street

### STREETPEOPLE

Not my fault

### MRS WALPURGIS

The running feet

STREETPEOPLE *exit.*

### MRS WALPURGIS

[*Sung.*] There's a body inside this shell
A heart beats behind the armour
Flesh moves beneath the crust
The carapace that shields my ardour

### MR CLIPBOARD

Not my fault

### MRS WALPURGIS

Despise the deviant

MR CLIPBOARD

Not my fault

MRS WALPURGIS

A political expedient

*Blackout.*

## Scene 2

*The street.* MRS WALPURGIS *is leafletting on the street.* NARRATOR *is watching her.*

NARRATOR

Morning, Mrs Walpurgis!

MRS WALPURGIS

Do I know you?

NARRATOR

Saw you in the local rag.
Your picture's everywhere.
The clean-up action plan.

MRS WALPURGIS

I don't think ...

NARRATOR

Well, you know, I'm a resident too.
I sit here and mind my business
most of the day [*points to peepshow*]
and sometimes it does get busy.
I hate standing around
with nothing to do. They say
the devil makes work for idle hands.

MRS WALPURGIS *exits hurriedly.*

NARRATOR

Goodbye Mrs W!

[*Pause.*]


I went to school for a while
there with her, but she doesn't
remember me. Of course,
we've both changed a lot since then.
Finished up in the same town,
opposite ends of the spectrum.
I know her daughter, though –
comes every year to the Pride Parade
giving out holy medals,
thinks we need a miracle
swooning saints on gilt-edged cards
promising discount on purgatory.
What can you say?
It's a free country.


NARRATOR *withdraws.* ANGEL *enters. A* CLIENT *enters and falls into step
with* ANGEL.

ANGEL

What's happening?

CLIENT

How much?

ANGEL

It's going to be a nice day
wouldn't you say?

CLIENT

I wouldn't know about that.

Now how much? I haven't got
much time to spare.

ANGEL

You've got a nice voice. I like
hearing you speak.

CLIENT

I need relief.

ANGEL

I understand. Relief
is what I give. Fifty
for a hand job, eighty
for the tongue and lips.
One-twenty for the whole bit.

[CLIENT *takes calculator from pocket.*]

Time is essence,
so to speak.

CLIENT

My boss is always
saying something similar.
I'd like her
to relieve me
but there's no chance
of that . . .

ANGEL

I'll be your boss.

CLIENT

You're not dressed for it.

ANGEL

Then close your eyes

and I'll clothe myself
in whatever you want.

                          CLIENT
I can't wait.
Time is of . . .

                          ANGEL
the essence. Move on down
the road. I'll catch you up.

BOTH *exit.*


## Scene 3

MRS WALPURGIS's *house. Monologue of* MRS WALPURGIS *to a group of*
RESIDENTS *who enter as* ANGEL *and* CLIENT *exit in previous scene.*

                     MRS WALPURGIS
There's something in the static,
in the dots on the television screen
between channels, before the test
pattern. And God speaks
between the notes
of Kenny G, I hear him,
it's not a cliché.
Christ was a handsome man
and loved all his children.
He redeemed that slut Mary,
but I know she was the only one.
Since my husband's death
I've kept my body intact –
it doesn't embarrass me
to talk about it. I wear
a bra to bed and my breasts
are firm and sharp.

They're all connected,
these papers. A photo shoot
for the community rag –
a stepping stone
to the holy grail.
A moral paper, this is not
a sacrilege. See, I think about
every implication.

In the beginning was the word.
The state paper is dedicated
to prising out evil
in the public interest.
It takes a stout heart.
It sees the brilliant aura
of our leader,
his Christian spirit
shining through
every tough decision.
It never lets them go.
That harlot looking innocent
on the front cover!
It's not long before
I replace her: from darkness
to light. My dark hair
is not a hindrance,
it still has lustre.

[MR CLIPBOARD *enters and gives each* RESIDENT *a "plate" before exiting.*]

Would you like some sponge?
A muffin or two?
Thank you, do.

RESIDENTS
[*They share these following lines – sung*]

Carbohydrates dampen ardour
make your will and temper harder

set your mind to stamp out evil
every nook and every cranny
squeaky clean and sharp and canny
no more slut or handsome devil
everything is on the level

MRS WALPURGIS
No! It won't harm your ulcer, it's quite bland.

Cooking keeps idle hands
from temptation

everyone in the area knows me,
the butcher keeps the best cuts
behind the counter, a signifier
in any community

[RESIDENTS, *with fixed smiles, giggle.*]

the youngest lambs
grace the plates
of my guests,
more tender
than what they serve
at receptions
and festivals.

[RESIDENTS, *with fixed smiles, giggle.*]

It is essential
we set the standards –
right down to what we eat,
how we groom
and deport ourselves.
This is for the children
I saw that slut Angel
near the school
the other day.

Heading for Smith Street.
She makes her way
right past the playground –
back from Oaken Park
where she takes her clients.
They let her place her mouth
around their appendages
without protection.

[RESIDENTS *gasp*.]

We now have a new law
to stop that.
Aids is everywhere.
Smith Street
is full of it,
I don't doubt.
We've more than
our fair share
of homosexuals here.

[RESIDENTS *gasp*.]

But first things first.
little by little.
step by step.

[RESIDENTS *exit*. ANGEL *appears upstage behind* MRS WALPURGIS. *She is
watching* MRS WALPURGIS. *She isn't spying, she's just there, hovering. She
sees everything, but it's as if she stares right through* MRS WALPURGIS, *deep
into the audience*.]

Well, that was a great success,
though I wish Mrs Hymenie
would eat her cake
over her plate,
she leaves such a mess.
I can see

they're all thinking
my way. They just needed
a spark. A leader.

[*Pause.*]

It's like herding cattle.

[*Laughs.*]

I shouldn't laugh.

Time to relax
With serepax!

*She turns to exit upstage and starts, and screams, upon noticing* ANGEL.

ANGEL
Lovely dress you're wearing.

MRS WALPURGIS
A Grace Brothers special.

[*To audience, as* ANGEL *exits.*]

The try-on wear-out
kind of shopping!
I deserve it. If they
ever found out, they
couldn't touch me. I do so much
for the community.

MRS WALPURGIS *exits.*

## Scene 4

*The street.* ANGEL *and* JACK *enter.*

JACK
I dreamt about you last night, Angel.

ANGEL
That's because you won't touch me, Jack.

JACK
You know it's the dirt, Angel.
The dripping taps. The stoves
left on when we've been spotting.

ANGEL
In your dream I became something else?

JACK
Yes, something else.

ANGEL
What?

JACK
I don't know really.
A bird of some sort.
A water bird. Picking
at the carcass of a cow.
Eating her insides out.

ANGEL
That's your guilt
for eating cows, Jack.

ANGEL *exits.*

What is it with these birds?
I dreamt of parrots on a farm:

a Nissen hut of netting
designed to keep the parrots out
that trapped a pair of twenty-eights:
vingt-huit, vingt-huit, vingt-huit,

[PROSTITUTES *enter and form line.* JACK *"works" his way among them.*]

a French colony, historic,
like the closing of brothels in Roe Street
or the surveillance
and vigilantes here in Smith Street –
the new phoneboxes without
glass walls, citizens
with notepads hoping
for kerbcrawlers, spitting

at your sort – refined varieties
in gardens that won't tolerate
trampling, the "wandering about"
roughing it on the edge

of salinity, or in lingo,
making a go of it,
despite the gentrification,
the naming, the lists

bred from a new mathematics.
A storm struck hard
in the summer, and that's why
the netting lifted. The parrots'

panopticon of colours
looking for an out –

extra-spectra, safe in the open,
the daylight, their language.

NARRATOR

[*Emerging from her shop.*]

Fancy words from a fancy man.
Jack of all trades and master of none
except Angel. Jack, be nimble, be quick,
the tricks are few and far between
they're cleaning up and driving out
and what will you do to earn a crust
when the Tuscan splendour's all there is
and the girls go back to school?
Who'll be your mainstay then?

JACK

Always got a trick
up my sleeve, darling,
they're not going to get
the better of me; actually,
I've just tripped over
a few dozen stereos –
could be a few bucks
in it for both of us . . .

NARRATOR

Ah Jack, your deals are always
such big deals! I've heard your talk before.

JACK

And don't you love it –
I'll get you on board
one of these days. Shit!

[PROSTITUTES *exit hurriedly.*]

Looks like a pig wagon.
Angel's out on a date ...
Hope she doesn't roll up
while they're sniffing about.

NARRATOR
Yeah, it'd only be the hundredth time
they've been up and down today. They reckon
your game is a mug's game ...

JACK
Genetically modified organisms.
Transgenic pigs. Always seen myself
as the head of a nature cult –
we could use some of your
bondage stuff and make them
feel at home. Look, it's
a Mexican standoff. Mexicans
make great cop movies.
Something of the Cars
that Ate Paris going
on here as well.
An Aussie flavour.
Gee, I love the movies.

NARRATOR
Don't go that often myself. Some of us
got work to do. But there's a film fest
coming up at the Rainbow Centre ... not
your cup of tea!

JACK
Ah, the dialogics of fucking.
Like my vocabulary, fancy, you say –
useful for judges. Makes a difference
if you've got cultural references
at your fingertips. And a private
school education. Singapore.

I've got what you might call
cachet. Mix it with street cred
and I'm a star. Don't need to
punch my girls around,
they worship me. I'm a god.

NARRATOR

I'm an atheist myself. No desire
to get down on my knees.
But hey, I hope you have a few thunderbolts
up your sleeve – you might just need them.
Those cops aren't exactly godfearing types.
And speaking of things heavenly, there's
your lady . . .

NARRATOR *exits.*

JACK

Shit! and there's a client
about to make a swoop,
I'd better catch her eye
before she hooks him
– there's no way
she'll see the cops
from there . . .

ANGEL *and* CLIENT *enter.*

CLIENT

Let's take a walk.

*They fall into step.*

ANGEL

Where are you parked?

CLIENT

At the end of the street.

COPS *enter.*

COP 1

Soliciting.

CLIENT *panics. Starts denying it.*

ANGEL

He's a friend.

CLIENT

[*Confused.*] I'm not. I mean, yes . . .

COP 2

Cut the crap.

JACK

What's the problem, officer?

COP 2

Piss off, or you'll go too.

COPS *walk* ANGEL *upstage.* ALL *freeze.*

NARRATOR

[*Voice off.*]

Watch this space.
Each patch and fetish a
pitch to stopper it, each
posture to quiet it,
loud mouth
this flag this red rag as it
moves tenuously
protected
like Ruth singing
"cover me, cover me

[98]

extend the border of your mantle over me" –
freedom would be
oblivion or
possession of it.

[ALL *exit.*]

Watch this space.

*Blackout.*

# Act 2

## Scene 1

*The street.* NARRATOR *enters.* ANGEL *enters, with* PROSTITUTES − *like a bodyguard.*

NARRATOR
Good to see you back again.

ANGEL
Oh yeah, a spell in the lock-up,
a cavity search, and I'm a new woman.

NARRATOR
Cavity search. Open season on any woman.
She said love your cunt not lumber
it around like hunger. Nobody else
will, remember, forgotten how. Poor
Miranda, no other treasure. Eye for a
bargain, eye for an eye. You can let them
in there, they won't find a thing. She said
seize back the means, they try to
privatise but you can put it out there. What
does it have in common with a 747. What
needst thou have more covering and
so on. She said Lady . . .

NARRATOR, ANGEL, PROSTITUTES
. . . love your cunt,

NARRATOR

but Fred Nile is in touch with the beating
heart of Australia and police
can authorise a nurse or a doctor I assure
you it has no nerve endings and on the
screen, worn as the battered aperture
of an old camera the dusk and "soft musk of her hollows"
the doctor is awed before. Imaging such
dilation. Stainless, like steel.

ANGEL

They went close to something.
I can feel it. You don't need
nerve endings. I vomited
in the morning.

NARRATOR

Behold the handmaid of the world.

ANGEL

Be it done to me according to the word.

PROSTITUTES *exit.*

NARRATOR

So how long are you going
to work this street. Surely
it's time to move on?
There are riper pickings
on the other side of town,
or maybe around Fremantle.

ANGEL

This street is ordered confusion.
The high-rise flats mean the yuppies
won't win out entirely − see,
don't stereotype me.

[*During the following* TWO PROSTITUTES *cross stage from opposite sides and "slash"* ANGEL's *face with lipstick and exit.* TWO OTHER PROSTITUTES *cross stage and slap/smudge* ANGEL's *face, and exit.*]

I don't wallow in the filth
or float ethereally;
no Manichaean take
on council rates.
I've worn wigs
and sat in on meetings.
So excited to have a new face
they didn't even recognise
their nemesis. And I got
that idea from Star Trek.


NARRATOR
Boldly going where no man has gone before!
Do you know what I do with their leaflets?
I wipe my arse with them.
It's called recycling.
Don't you worry, they won't stop
at anything. They only tolerate me because
I pay rates: prime location
in the middle of town. But don't put it past them,
they're into purgation.


ANGEL
If I let them contain me
and my cavities, they'd
fill me anally and love it.
I'm good for profit,
and the mining industry
likes that. It's just more gold
to give away.


JACK *enters.* NARRATOR *withdraws and watches from a distance.*

ANGEL

Jack, you're my man.

JACK

I'm nobody's man.

ANGEL

You're a man's man.
A blokey bloke.

JACK

What are you implying?

ANGEL

That you like your body.
I know you work out.

JACK

What's it to you?

ANGEL

Words don't work for this.
We provide for each other.

ANGEL *and* JACK *take up parodic tango drop position.* ANGEL *starts caressing* JACK *but this turns into a search inside his coat.*

JACK

I am a creative person.
I am your agent. A spiritual
mentor, a physical protector.

ANGEL

A provider. You are
my programme.
We counsel
each other.

JACK

But I don't need you, Angel.

[JACK *drops* ANGEL *and moves away.* NARRATOR *crosses to help* ANGEL.]

I'll do okay when our
partnership breaks up.
In fact, I'm thinking
of registering
for the small business
incentive scheme.
I've got a plan.

NARRATOR

Jack, the man with the plan.

JACK

Butt out of it.

JACK *and* ANGEL *exit.* STREETPEOPLE *enter simultaneously with* MRS WALPURGIS *and* MR CLIPBOARD.

STREETPEOPLE

[*Shared lines.*]

There's that bitch

There's that shit

There's the vigilante clutch

The god-blessed creep who runs this street

The god-sucked geek who whacks his meat

Who blocks her snatch

Who ties his cock

Put cling wrap round their private parts

Pull up the sheets and sniff their farts

Put shit upon the queens and tarts

Take notes on those upon the street

Live lives unblessed by joy and grief

[Rhythm change]

Live their lives in a ditch

Upstanding cits

Upstanding what?

Upstanding shits

Upstanding what?

Upstanding ...

ALL

So high

phallic monuments ...

ALL

So low

to perverted ...

ALL

So down

visions.

ALL

Go down.

STREETPEOPLE *"go down" into a tangled and writing heap on the stage
and remain there as lights change into next scene.*

## Scene 2

*In* MRS WALPURGIS*'s house.* MR CLIPBOARD *and* MRS WALPURGIS.
STREETPEOPLE *watching them.*

MRS WALPURGIS

Street scum!

MR CLIPBOARD

Street scum!

MRS WALPURGIS

Where is there restraint?

MR CLIPBOARD

Where is their restraint?

BOTH

[*Chant.*] We work
We work
We prosper
We smirk

MR CLIPBOARD

We take the moral high ground

MRS WALPURGIS

We see the scum around
inhabiting the street
their dopey drug-led feet

[106]

MR CLIPBOARD

Their vacant smiling stares
They haven't any cares

MRS WALPURGIS

Where is there restraint?

MR CLIPBOARD

Where is their restraint?

[MRS WALPURGIS *and* MR CLIPBOARD *stroke and fondle their own bodies before and during the following song.*]

[*Sung.*] I hear what you are saying
your words fill me with glee
I gaze upon your body
so strong, so pure, so free

MRS WALPURGIS

Pervert!

MR CLIPBOARD

Street scum!

STREETPEOPLE *laugh, make insulting gestures, and exit. Pause.*

MR CLIPBOARD

I saw her at it again. Not the morning,
she's working the dusk. Kids were still
out and about. She was wearing
hardly a stitch. You could see
her bottom. I got some numbers,
even in the half-light. And one bloke
went for a mother and her daughter.
I got his number and he almost
ran me down. The surprise, the fear
on his face gave me a pleasant shiver.

### MRS WALPURGIS

I'm glad you're so committed,
but we must remember
this is not about us – it's about
the community. Our daughters, especially.
It's a fine line, Mr Clipboard, a fine line.
I shudder to think. I try not to.
I focus on what can be done.
Faith without works is dead, that's what
the apostle says.


### MR CLIPBOARD

I see myself as being
in the vanguard, not a mere disciple.
I want to set a good example,
to be remembered for my works.


### MRS WALPURGIS

But works of course are not enough. As it says
in Hebrews –


### MR CLIPBOARD

You photograph well, Mrs Walpurgis.
There was another shot of you
by the corner phone booth.
Funny watching them
try and huddle under
the wind shelter now.
Puts a bit of a damper on things.


### MRS WALPURGIS

Yes, well, those with nothing to hide
have nothing to be afraid of. I've always kept
an open house myself.


### MR CLIPBOARD

When we've sorted this problem out,
we'll have to look to the Aboriginals

that hang about. This stuff about
tribal meeting places is so out-of-date.
School kids play footy
on that oval where they gather.
Another lot we should move on quickly.
Just watch the property prices go up!

MRS WALPURGIS
You should read He wants us to Prosper,
Mr Clipboard. The Lord
likes abundance, you're a man
after His own heart.

MR CLIPBOARD
Yes, Mrs Walpurgis,
I like to be well fed.

MRS WALPURGIS
Abundance! "The earth
is the Lord's and the fulness thereof" –
doesn't say anything about
them now does it? Heaven helps those
who . . .

MR CLIPBOARD
[Chiming in with her.] . . . help themselves.

SFX – bell sounds, lighting change.

## Scene 3

Near the belltower. JACK calls and COPS enter.

JACK
Hey boys! What do you think
of the new belltower?

A bit of a prick
with a bunch of bells –
must have been exposed
to radiation at a young age.

COP 1

You know us Jack,
we won't take this crap.
Shut it while your luck's in.

JACK

Now, now, I'm your friend.
You like my girls, they
keep their mouths shut
and make you spend spend spend!

COP 2

This guy's getting to me.
He's full of it.

JACK

Just shootin' off my mouth . . .

[*They rough him up.*]

Fuck off! Keep the hands to yourself.
I'm telling you, I've got friends.
And some of your park-dwelling habits
would be of great interest to them!

COP 1

Your friends in the press
have had a sock put in it:
one of ours
is holding the reins now.
And he's going to hang you high,
Jack boy. A tongue-lashing
with bite!

Jack and the belltower.
We should send him up there.

                    JACK
And what? Chop it to the ground
before I get down?

                    COP 2
This sounds like blasphemy.
The tower is a beacon for posterity.

                    JACK
I sold a stereo
and a car radio
to a labourer
who drank beer
by the river
after a hard day's work
on the holy tower.
He said that after a few
it was true,
as rumour has it,
that no one could understand
what the others were saying.

JACK *exits.*

                    COP 2
A holy place. Holy places
do that to you.

*Sound of a phone ringing. Or,* COPS *"vibrate" before taking mobile phones
from pockets. The two* COPS *speak in turns, as if automated.*

                    COP 1
And which street was it on?

COP 2

And you were walking home from work.

COP 1

Well yes Ma'am, I'm sorry to have to say this,

COP 2

and I don't mean it as an insult,

COP 1

but it's likely he took you for . . . [*pause*]

COP 2

Just because you were in the area.

COPS

[*Together, as if chanting.*] If you ring our hotline, we can have someone out there within five minutes to remove him.

COPS *exit.*

## Scene 4

*Courtroom.* NARRATOR, ANGEL, *and* JACK. SFX. *Wind, hellfire, lighting effects. The following shouted as though on the deck of a ship during a storm.*

NARRATOR

Angel, you know something
that might work in your defence:
if the hand of those who condemn you
is caught in the till,
things will be easier.

ANGEL

I see a lot of things,
but what binds me

is stronger than
the hippocratic oath.
A lawyer must respect
the confidentiality
of his client. It's a contract.

NARRATOR

Election promises are made,
few are kept.

PROSTITUTES *enter with tables,* CLIENT *with chair. After placing they take
up positions in "court".*

JACK

Listen to her, Angel,
she's been there before.

ANGEL

Do you want me about, Jack?

JACK

It's not that, it's just
you score well for me.
You keep us both happy.

ANGEL

You're a romantic, Jack.

MAGISTRATE *enters, with* COPS *and* MRS WALPURGIS *and* MR CLIP-
BOARD. *SFX cease.* ANGEL *stands before* MAGISTRATE.

MAGISTRATE

Do you like publicity, young lady?

ANGEL

I didn't ask to be photographed.
Those cameras
are embarrassing my family.

MAGISTRATE

You're embarrassing your family,
let's get this right.


ANGEL

You're making my problems
their problems.


MAGISTRATE

I see that you've been
on the methadone programme before.


ANGEL

'Done doesn't work for me.
It's bad art.


MAGISTRATE

It's bad art or jail.
And you know the new law.
It's just a matter of how much jail.
You've confessed your guilt.


JACK

[*Yelling out.*] Mitigating circumstances!


MAGISTRATE

Enough.


ANGEL

[*As if in tongues. SFX under.*]


Up-flow spreads and hazes
the spaces between buildings,
the step of a mother and her child
is loud behind me; it's you,
in the accusative, the princess
and the pea, the hoaxes

performed brightly
in peasant's garb. I'm
central European. We are
parallel notations. Script.
The sounds between the notes.
The dust collects
in make-up during the summer months.
Clients like the stiff-nippled cold.
Inquisitor. Purple. The monochrome
businesses that fuel, ad nauseam.
The furies are contained
neatly. A register. Signatures.
Income tax.

*SFX cease.*

                              JACK
Tell her, Angel, tell her
what you saw! Angel sees things,
your Honour. And she can
get inside people's dreams.
But she's discreet,
and only goes where she's wanted.

                        MAGISTRATE
Enough from you.
One more crack and that's it.

[*Pause.*]

Now, Angel, what's
this gentleman
talking about?

                           ANGEL
I see things, your Honour,
but it's not for me
to say what I see.

MAGISTRATE

Well, you're under oath
and I expect the truth.

ANGEL

I'm not sure
if this is to do with truth,
your Honour.
But if you consider
the court a gallery,
we could hang pictures.

PROSTITUTES *giggle.*

MAGISTRATE

That sounds vaguely contemptuous,
but I'll let it go.
Don't forget you need a few
grains of sand
in your favour.

ANGEL

What I see is nothing, really.
People just think loudly.

MAGISTRATE

If offered a jail sentence
or a court order for rehabilitation
which would you take?

JACK

[*Yelling out.*] Watch those preferences –
they'll always be given
to those who do you
the most damage.

One more time, and that's it!
Silence.

ANGEL *shifts across to* MAGISTRATE. *Wooing him/her.*

ANGEL

Jack is right, your Honour.
The people you've driven out
from the city, the concrete
blurring their meeting places
and the by-laws moving them on.
The preferences go to those
who'd make their lives harder.
The blood that flows through my cunt
grows louder and louder.
My clients ask me if I practise yoga.

MAGISTRATE *has moved to be near* ANGEL. *Intimately.*

MAGISTRATE

Don't think I don't know a spell
when I hear it! We do in-service
courses for things like this.
I am an amateur photographer –
don't you love that word . . .
amateur amateur amateur . . .

[ALL *repeat "amateur" several times, descending into sotto voce*]

I know how to capture the moment.
Carpe diem. But I'm not ready
to make a martyr of you yet.
And watch the language,
your vocab's pushing the envelope.
Do you believe in fate.
As flies to wanton . . . girls?

ANGEL

Sometimes I feel like the whole street
is flowing through my body.
I can hear the sweet words,
the arguments, television sets.

MAGISTRATE

Sometimes I get that feeling up here.
The river flows through me.
I sail at twilight.
The cormorants hunch
on the pylons and jetties.
The landfill brings an intensity
to what's left. I don't
know what I mean, but preservation
is a decision. The night heron
lives in colonies. I see
a lone heron stalking.
I see one near the old brewery.
Birds alive in the darkness.
Is this what you're saying?

*Pause.*

ANGEL

It is, your honour.
It is.

*Pause.*

NARRATOR

There's a link been forged here.
He feels for her. The sentence
will be harsh.

MAGISTRATE *moves back behind table.*

Six months.

[ALL *gasp. For some it's too long, for others, it is not long enough.*]

Suspended.

[ALL *sigh, some with relief – some with exasperation.*]

But only because
something's in the air.

NARRATOR

Could it be
politicians' promises?

ALL *express surprise, then exit other than* PROSTITUTES.


PROSTITUTES
[*Sharing the following lines – perhaps while shifting tables etc. off stage.*]

The street plays the game

It always looks the same

It stretches to the north
and the south

It is so very strange
it's hard to rearrange

I stand here with my hands and my mouth

With my hands and my mouth.

[*Rhythm change.*]

I left home
my mother beat me

I left home
my father fucked me

I left home
and hit the street

How romantic!

*Rhythm change.* CLIENT *enters.* PROSTITUTES *share lines.*

CLIENT
Where's the place that I can score?

PROSTITUTES
Where's the hit?

Where's the store?

CLIENT
Where's the man?

PROSTITUTES
I'm waiting . . .

Where's the hand?

I'm waiting . . .

Where's the mouth?

I'm waiting . . .

And, where's the hole?

So coy!

PROSTITUTES *seize* CLIENT *and lift him up.*

CLIENT

Where's the way out of here?

JACK

[*Voice off.*] Who wants out?

PROSTITUTES *exit, carrying* CLIENT.

# Act 3

## Scene 1

*The street.* ANGEL *enters.*

ANGEL

It all passes through me,
as if the myth fits the form.
The Master Basho
would make a haiku of me.
Your private spaces
are made public
through my body.
I am a concept. I am a snail
that carries my home –
my mouth, my cunt,
my arsehole,
around with me.
I am on your front lawn,
your doorstep,
in your letter box,
slipped through your front door.
Piled high in the newsagency.
I am spit in the eye
of Pauline Hanson.
I am the dirt under
the fingernails
of parliamentary
committees.
I am the film
on the teeth

of the health department.
I am nicotine. I am alcohol.
I am an absolute point on the spectrum.

NARRATOR *enters.*

NARRATOR

Out there where the only steps
are sharp or jazz-tango, bit
between his teeth and he'll
have his head or death of, safe
in that alabaster chamber your
cold bed/fast bolt/bills mount
you hold out for a way will make
an honest woman of him yet.
Red-eyed in the red light.
Roll model, the only spring
you'll trigger a bedspring.
Count every muscle, Ophelia
practise with lulls in traffic that pelvic
floor the one floor you'll ever hold
limp as excuses and a hobbled
walk. Because you're mine/I keep
a close watch, walk the skirt the
verge of something a break-
through like in love for the very
first time, the fixed foot brings them
home like fetishists, lean and hearken
so I bend where I lonely began.

*They dance a tango.*

ANGEL

Where do I begin
and end? My limits
the city limits.

NARRATOR

The city is a body.
The body eats itself.

[*The tango stops.*]

Using this model
you might think
running a peepshow
belongs to the anatomy
of excrement.
But this body is Frankenstein,
genetically modified: there's
no logic as to how it's put together.
Unlike Adelaide or Canberra,
planned cities made
without convict labour,
Perth's hydraulics run
on different pressures.
So here I stand,
doorkeeper to a cybernetic
melodrama.

ANGEL

Or a spiritual story,
a transcendental tale,
a dialogue of humours.
Plants with special properties
that might heal or comfort
lungs, stomach, heart,
left behind in the rush
for synthetics. Out there – diminished –
the hakea, dryandra, grevillea,
names stripped of their growth,
a place in language. They grow on the roadsides,
in the parks, in the streets.
Full of fluid I let them fill
the spaces I save for myself.

They can't understand this.
It's not to do with anything good
or bad, it's just the case that is.
The parks and the gardens –

NARRATOR

and the universities
are our Walden Ponds:
out there, discovering
the limits and satisfactions
of the body.

ANGEL

Solitary.

NARRATOR

Thinking about community.
We are all parents and children
of this hybridised body.

NARRATOR *and* ANGEL *exit – with lingering eyelines to each other.*
PARLIAMENTARY DELEGATION *enters and does "song and dance" routine*
*to following.*

PARLIAMENTARY DELEGATION

We're a parliamentary delegation
sent here to spy out deviation
To regulate against the whores
with their nasty habits
and filthy sores
to clean the dealers off the street
In itself that's no mean feat

We're a parliamentary delegation
sent here to spy out deviation
To regulate what's right and wrong
To lock some up

move others along
to clear the riffraff off the street
put bombs beneath their feet

We're a parliamentary delegation
sent here to spy out deviation
We're sent by the powers that be
to root out filth
to set you free
to cleanse and clean and clear the streets
Keep naughty business between the sheets.

*Repeat of first two lines before marching off without sound, other than "fascist" footfalls.*

## Scene 2

*In* MRS WALPURGIS's *house.* COPS, MR CLIPBOARD, *and* MRS WALPURGIS.

COP 1

[*To* MR CLIPBOARD.]

We checked out that plate
you took down last week:
the kerbcrawler
chatting up the mother.
It was his wife, the child
you mention was his daughter.
They park their car
out front everyday.

COP 2

Zealous. Very zealous.

COP 1

You're not going
to help the case
by being too enthusiastic.
Fortunately the newspaper
isn't interested
in the family's complaints.

COP 2

Doesn't sell newspapers.

MRS WALPURGIS

We mustn't criticise
Mr Clipboard,
he's on the front line.
Friendly fire
it's called. This is a war,
make no mistake,
and all wars
have collateral
damage.

Look down this street.
I've seen gangs of youth
with spray cans
in broad daylight
putting their marks
on the bright wash
of architect-designed
houses. How are we going to
attract the professionals
if that keeps up?

And I've seen her
chatting with them
and handing out cigarettes –
a crime in itself,
tobacco to minors.

She should be locked
up for that anyway.

MR CLIPBOARD

The word. Graffiti. Signatures.

COP 1

What's he on about?

MRS WALPURGIS

Shell shock. He's under stress.
We need to support him.

COP 2

I was shot at once.
The guy who tried to plug me
was a doctor. Had put a bullet
in his wife in a blind rage.

MR CLIPBOARD

[*Dreamily.*] She talks to me while I take down numbers.
Sometimes I feel like she's family.

MRS WALPURGIS

Come on Mr Clipboard,
it's time you were
getting back to your post.

MR CLIPBOARD

Yes, there's a lot of cars,
a lot of number plates.
a lot of numbers
to be taken down.
Recorded.

MR CLIPBOARD *exits.*

COP 2

He's got a problem.
An unreliable witness.

COP 1

His observations don't add up.
Doesn't work as data.

MRS WALPURGIS

He is a powerful symbol.
A neighbourhood icon.
In the vanguard.
A martyr.

COPS *exit.*

MRS WALPURGIS

He is a powerful symbol.
A neighbourhood icon.
In the vanguard.
A martyr.

MRS WALPURGIS *exits.*

## Scene 3

*Interior of squat.* NARRATOR, JACK, *and* ANGEL. *As* NARRATOR *begins speaking,* ANGEL *goes into labour and eventually gives birth.*

NARRATOR

Smith Street stretches
from Lowland to Mount Regulation.
It cruises past park territory,
the Tuscan splendours.
The squats where vigilantes
oust mothers and kids,

"wallowing among the filth",
drug paraphernalia, dirty knickers
and used condoms.
They think so hard about it
the place arranges itself
perfectly for them.
Their polluted minds
open up.
Wire out the poor.
No squatters. Neat ones
are the greatest threat. Moving in
as if nothing's happening.
Taking over. Upsets
the balance. The belltower
needs the taxes.


                              JACK

Look! The head's appearing
out of Angel's darkness.
It's like the night
is unfurling.
The sun's up
and it's midnight.
Why is she screaming!?


                        NARRATOR
It's a different kind of opening.
She needs a place to bring it up.


                              JACK
We'll tear down the wire,
we'll dig the garden.
We'll polish the kitchen tiles.
Repair the verandah.
We'll stake a claim,
we'll open our doors,
we'll make community.
My brothers

will be godfathers.
The sisters will be godmothers.
The displaced will wander by
and bless their child
in their own language.
The state won't have enough money
to evict us. We'll invite
the newspaper
for the baby photos.
We'll sing our lungs out.

MAGISTRATE

[*Entering.*] This is justice!
We'll sing
as if our lives
depend on it!

ALL *enter during following.*

NARRATOR

So we sing for the people of Smith Street.
We sing for the coppers. We sing for the court.
We sing for the Liberals who send out
surveys and spout prayers against debauchery.
We sing for Mr Clipboard and Mrs Walpurgis,
we recognise the belltower
as the true meeting of art and spirit:

ALL

[*Singing, first to the tune of "Ding Dong Bell", and then to the tune of Monty Python's "Every Sperm is Sacred". During this,* ANGEL *walks downstage with "baby/bundle".*]

Big dong bell
Pussy's in the cell
We put in her in
Then we'll let her out

What a naughty boy was that
To try to win our vote like that
Clean the streets by changing laws
And promise us a sunset clause . . .

Every womb is sacred
Every womb the State
If a womb gets wayward
Court can legislate

[*Repeat.*] Every womb . . .

ALL *except* NARRATOR *exit* – *singing.*


### Scene 4

*The street.*

NARRATOR
From the third or fourth storey
of the apartment blocks, the city
glows in the afternoon heat.
The light is sweet, not fragmented
and variegated as down in the street.
And sound rises up into lyric,
and counter beat sets up harmony,
the wave motion sweeps
out toward the hills, resonating
like the skin of the eardrum.
Down here, the city
is just flesh. A body.
I celebrate mine,
others replace theirs.
Angel is an angel is an angel.
Her offspring is hungry.
Her milk never came.

I am lactating
in sympathy
and the baby
will have mine.

NARRATOR *exits.* COPS *enter and seize* CLIENT *as he enters.* COPS *pull a*
*mailbag over* CLIENT *and* COP 1 *lifts him onto shoulder in "fireman's lift".*

COP 1

How many crimes
will she get away with now?

COP 2

Let's send a baby photo
to the paper. The child of angel.
An archangel.

COP 1

You've got to have
a sense of humour
in this job.
Did you notice the light
when we went up to search that place
last night? The city lights.
As if night was alive,
without pollution.

COP 2

All light is pollution.

COP 1

I was brought up C of E.
I don't need to pretend
this kid's not mine.

                        COP 2
And I a Baptist.
I positively
deny it.

COP 1 *puts down* CLIENT.

                        COP 1
But we got into this
feeling we could make a difference.

                        COP 2
I used an enlargement method
from the back of a magazine
and it left me an object
of ridicule in the change rooms.

                        COP 1
I change on my own,
avoid the change rooms.

                        COP 2
I've always wanted a child.
Maybe this one will do.

                        COP 1
Ditto. But the brass
might suspect
conspiracy. Say
it's one of theirs.

                        COP 2
Well, if it's got
teeth and gold fillings
we'll know for sure.

[COP 1 *picks up* CLIENT *and exits.*]

Jesus, without Jack and Angel
we're out of a job.

COP 2 *exits.* NARRATOR *and* JACK *enter.*

NARRATOR
Something has happened to you, Jack.
You're well dressed, man – caring
for the girls has come a cropper.
Your dark side is showing.

JACK
It was always showing, O my purveyor
of eye candy and abjection,
just because I keep my fluids
locked in their tubes
and chambers, people don't
see it. I've got an idea, no more
of this sentimental shit.
This baby of Angel's
is my ticket out of here.
I've met this man
high up in the law, shall we say,
who'll pay anything – he can work
it; there'll be no legal comeback.
His wife's barren. She
draws babies on her stomach.
She puts plastic toys
into her cavity.
Angel is blasted.
She can't look after a child.
She sold it to me
before it popped
into her belly.

JACK *starts, as* ANGEL *appears, as if from above, in a blue light, like an apparition of the Virgin.*

The precipice, the waterfall,
faultlines and cracks in the surface,
broken fences, electric gates
swinging open onto cars,
traffic lights flicker,
headlights fray, blurred
on the edges the grass
struggles to hold back the concrete.

[*The blue light flickers into a scratchy video image of* ANGEL *across the backdrop.*]

I made television last night,
couldn't recognise myself,
even determined not to recognise
myself. They condemn me as failed
woman and mother and citizen
outright. No place on the census
for such flotsam and jetsam,
that sea of light flooding
out like filth from blocked drains.

NARRATOR
[*Pleading.*] What do you see?

ANGEL
Reporters and policeman and doctors
and nurses and health inspectors.
Councillors with hell problems
behind closed doors. I see in
and look on past. I see the blood
on my hands, pollution
where I walk. A red bird
sits where my heart is: my heart
is reliable because the red bird
always sits there, bobbing slightly.

                            JACK
Rehabilitation. Parole.

JACK *exits.*


                            ANGEL
They think I planned the birth
to keep them out of my heart-space.
Like they said with Lindy –
taking what little
she had left –
drew their mother's milk
and spat it back at her.
The film that rolls on like an oracle
I keep to myself. They fear
my prophecies.

                        NARRATOR
Where will you go?

                            ANGEL
A flight into Egypt,
a midnight flit.
Help me.


MAGISTRATE *enters with "baby" and places it in* ANGEL*'s arms.* NARRA-
TOR *moves toward* ANGEL *– the three forming a group together, with* ANGEL
*in the centre.*


                            ANGEL
It's the light in the hair
the camera remarked on.
My hair, the hair
I could almost believe was mine
if I let go, drifted
down the street
before breaking out
into the black light.

ANGEL, MAGISTRATE, *and* NARRATOR *exit.* PROSTITUTES *enter and form line.* JACK *enters and "picks" them up as he crosses.* PROSTITUTES *follow* JACK *off stage.* CLIENT *enters, sees everyone has gone. He takes up starting position under Belltower. Lights fade on him.*

**THE END**

# The Wasps

*A Dance Routine for Three Players*

Who that has Reason, and his Smell,
Wou'd not among Roses and Jasmin dwell?
— COWLEY

## Characters

BILL, *husband, pedantic, phobic, hypochondriac embassy worker*
SHIRLEY, *wife, New Ager, vegetarian, interested in spiritualism*
STAN, *exterminator*
SINGERS, *optional*

## The set, the play, the ritual

*Large house on the Thames (in Act 3, the "new" house set design can be based
on that of the "old" house). Actually very old but has been done up inside to
reflect Bill's taste for clean surfaces. A number of rooms – lounge, kitchen,
bedroom and balcony. Front door etc. The flat is sparsely furnished, and the set
should employ flat planar surfaces, though shelves and cupboard tops are
littered with Shirley's spiritualist and New Age bric-a-brac. Crystals, tarot
cards, etc. On at least one of the surfaces should be some erotic "primitivist"
art. Colours should be basic, and costumes all in one colour – red, black, and*

white – with participants changing colours for each act. Music is important. Medieval: choral voices gently singing Latin hymns with lute etc in the background, or just a soundtrack of instrumentation. Composers can be as late as Byrd. This is interspersed during the overt dancing scenes with either trance music (DJ Spooky etc) or psychedelic frenzy music (very early Pink Floyd – ie Syd Barrett compositions). The exterminator, Stan, should be in a toxic suit that changes colour in each act. He can wear a codpiece. This is optional. Stage directions are kept to a minimum to allow the text to create the necessary stage dynamic. The director should let it flow (as in the body without organs) as s/he pleases. Silences and pauses are not always marked, but the whole work is a dance – with the time lapse between the choreographed movements just still points in this interaction. It is ritualistic and "artificial". The accents of Shirley and Bill are more English than Australian. The wasps are not seen by the audience, but they can constantly be heard. The whole play is "choreographed".

# Act 1

*In the house. It is a warm day. Sun is streaming in through the curtains. A scratching noise in the roof and walls.*

## Scene 1

BILL *and* SHIRLEY *seated in the loungeroom.*

SHIRLEY

I read Mrs Wilberforce's cards today and they said that she's in for a big win.

BILL

Shirley, I've told you a million times, I don't want to know. What you do is your own business, but it's just mumbo-jumbo to me.

SHIRLEY

You should take an interest in my work, Bill.

BILL

It's not work, Shirley, it's just a hobby. The library is your work.

SHIRLEY

Well, I'm getting more and more clients all the time and it won't be long before I can quit the library.

BILL

[*Alarmed.*] Shirley, you can't do that, we need the money, we need the security. And think what the twins' friends would say – it's embarrassing enough already for them, with all this claptrap you have around the house. [*He cocks an ear and frowns.*] Listen . . . listen, can you hear a scratching, buzzing sound? It's that scratching we've been hearing for months, but it's something else as well. A buzzing sound.

SHIRLEY

Like a bee? No, I can't hear it. I can't hear anything. It wouldn't be like that, Bill, and you shouldn't mock the powers. They can hear, you know.

BILL

I can hear as well, and I hear a buzzing sound. Listen!

SHIRLEY

Yes, I guess I can hear the scratching. That same old scratching sound, but it's so faint. The twins complain about it at night sometimes. Oh Bill! [*She clasps her hand to her mouth.*] . . .

BILL

[*Slightly alarmed.*] What, what is it . . .

SHIRLEY

I hope I haven't woken a dark spirit.

BILL

Jeez, Shirley, I don't know how I remain married to you.

SHIRLEY

[*Forgetting it as fast as she says it.*] Because you love me. . . ?

BILL

Well, I guess I do . . . for all your strange ways. [*He sneezes.*] Think I might be coming down with something. Have been feeling quite off-colour lately. There are draughts in this place. It's time I had a check-up.

SHIRLEY

It's only a month since your last visit to the doctor, Bill. You'll be bankrupting the National Health if you go too often!

#### BILL

[*Feeling indulged, making light of it.*] National Health, it's a joke really. I've been meaning to take out private health cover – it's important to be covered properly. Speaking of which, have you paid your life insurance? I notice a letter on the table from them . . .

#### SHIRLEY

Now, that's addressed to me, Bill, and not something you need to worry about.

#### BILL

Just trying to be helpful. [*He sneezes again.*] I tell you Shirley, I'm coming down with something!

#### SHIRLEY

I'll rub some oils into your chest later. [*Pause.*] Wonder what the twins are doing now?

#### BILL

Probably listening to the older kids telling scary stories. That's what always happens on camps.

#### SHIRLEY

I hate camp, I want them home.

#### BILL

They'll be home soon enough. We should take advantage of the privacy.

#### SHIRLEY

There's something I want to watch on the telly tonight. It's a programme about central Australia. I wish we'd gone to Uluru when Mum offered to take us years back.

#### BILL

Travelling with your mother would have been a nightmare. And for God's sake, don't be so pretentious, it's called Ayers Rock.

#### SHIRLEY

Then why do they tell you to call it Uluru at the embassy? It's more respectful, it is.

#### BILL

That's political, and no concern of yours.

#### SHIRLEY

Well, I'm going to call it Uluru, and that's that.

#### BILL

Whatever . . . I can still hear that buzzing sound. [*He looks around, then gets up and looks around the room carefully.*] Nothing – but I can hear it so clearly. Maybe I'm getting the flu. Your ears play funny tricks when a fever sets in. [*He tests his forehead.*] There, I feel a little clammy, maybe a little hot.

#### SHIRLEY

[*Testing his forehead.*] You're perfectly cool, Bill. Your cheeks are rosy and you look like you'd have a perfect bill of health.

#### BILL

[*Flustered.*] Well I can still hear that buzzing sound. And I feel as if I'm about to sneeze again . . .

*He sneezes.*

*Blackout.*


## Scene 2

*Next day.* BILL *and* SHIRLEY *in the bedroom.*

#### SHIRLEY

Take a look at this, Bill!

BILL

Can't it wait a minute? I'm doing something.

SHIRLEY

It's important.

BILL

Jeez, Shirley, it's always important. [*He wanders over.*] Shit! That's amazing. There must be a dozen of them.

SHIRLEY

Wonder why they're out there, it's so cold!

BILL

Must have been sleeping and then disturbed, maybe driven out of their place. [*Pause.*] I tell you what, I bet it's wasps we've been hearing in the wall cavities, in the roof. Kept me awake for ages last night. Worked their way into my nightmares. Dreaming without images, just the sound of scratching and all threats and confusions associated with it. I dreamt I imagined seeing things: claws, weapons, fingernails, but never actually saw anything or anyone. These walls are blanks. The ceiling is an impenetrable blank. Maybe the warmth yesterday woke them, and they're trying to make their way back in. And Shirley, I dreamt that you died. I dreamt that they filled you with poison and you turned red, then black. I couldn't recognise you anymore. It was horrible, it made me feel ill.

SHIRLEY

[*Laughing.*] You always dream that I'm dying, Bill. If it's not wasps, it's a car accident or the plague. [*She muses.*] Why don't they come back in the way they went out?

BILL

Maybe they're confused because of the sudden return of the cold weather – the chill has upset their radar.

SHIRLEY

I understand what that means, I'm feeling a little disorientated myself today. Thought we'd shaken winter, and it comes back stronger than before.

BILL

[*Moving away from the window, distracted.*] I've got this bloody committee meeting this evening. There's real tension between committee members over this safety issue in the embassy ballroom. I mean, it's got to be confronted, it's not going to go away. It's the expense more than anything, but I can't see the market rising much in the foreseeable future, and the money problems aren't going to go away. We should just fix it and move on.

SHIRLEY

[*Still staring through the window.*] They're angry but fading. Really frustrated. But the cold's eating them. I think they're paper wasps. No, European Wasps. Yes, that's what they are. I saw pictures of them in Australia. They're vermin, you know. Dangerous pests. The agricultural and environmental people fight hard to keep them out. They come in on planes and ships and in people's clothes. Don't they lay eggs inside spiders? Can't recall. I was stung on my inside leg when I was a teenager. Swelled up something shocking. I had an allergic reaction. Too many of them and I'd be dead. That was in Australia. There are warnings out all over the place in Perth: keep an eye out, beware the European Wasps. They swarm. Their communities are strong and indifferent. They can kill. They are a notifiable offence.

BILL

I suppose I should do some politicking and push the point.

SHIRLEY

We've got to let them in, Bill. We can't just let them die!

BILL

What? Let them in? Don't be daft. They'd kill us. Dirty things, let them freeze to death.

SHIRLEY

That's cruel, Bill!

#### BILL

[*Shifting his attention.*] That's the buzzing, there must be one of them inside. How long do they live? I don't want any filthy insect inside. It's disgusting. You can't bring up kids in a house full of flying, crawling things.

#### SHIRLEY

That was a distressed spirit you heard.

#### BILL

How would you know? You didn't even hear it.

#### SHIRLEY

I felt it. [*Pause.*] The wasps wouldn't die in Australia, it's warm there. I miss the warmth sometimes, Bill.

#### BILL

They would die, the public health people would be onto them. Like starlings.

#### SHIRLEY

Depends which part of Australia, though. They'd die in winter in Tasmania, it gets cold there. But I'd miss the old place, if I went back. It's so old, behind the walls. Maybe three hundred years old. It's rich in spirits.

#### BILL

[*Puffing himself up.*] It's important for some of us to be here, to keep the links with the old country strong. It's about respect.

#### SHIRLEY

I hate Australia.

#### BILL

Don't speak like that, Shirley. It's unforgivable.

*Fade out.*

## Scene 3

BILL *and* SHIRLEY *in the bedroom.*

### BILL

[*Yelling offstage, very upset and even terrified.*] They're bloody everywhere. Where have they come from? It feels like they're under my skin!

### SHIRLEY

[*Drying her hair.*] I've been talking to them for an hour. I've used a jar to catch some and let them go outside. It's a warmer day and they shouldn't die. They're tiny spirits of all who have lived in the area. It's such an old area, so full of souls. Some of them have suffered, but others had happy lives. It takes all sorts.

### BILL

[*Appearing at the door.*] You wanted them in yesterday! This is too much. I'll ring the pest people immediately. I hate insects.

### SHIRLEY

It was cold, too cold, yesterday. I'm so glad the twins are away. They wouldn't have understood.

### BILL

If they got stung by these monsters they'd be in hospital! You should watch yourself, you'll get stung and that'll be it – you said yourself you were allergic.

### SHIRLEY

It's early, they're kind of drowsy. You learn a lot by watching them. [*She pauses.*] I didn't think you were listening when I told you that.

### BILL

Where . . . how have they got in?

### SHIRLEY

[*Getting focussed.*] This place is riddled with cracks and holes. That's why it's so hard to heat. But it gives it character. No amount of clever decorating can make it what it's not.

BILL

I feel dirty.

SHIRLEY

The wasps have taken a liking to the rooms with big windows. Trying to get out. Trying to get in and out. It's quite confusing.

BILL

In the space of time we've been talking, they've doubled in numbers.

SHIRLEY

It's going to be a beautiful spring day. I think I will spend it outdoors. Don't feel like working today.

BILL

You have to work, we need the money. I'm going to ring the pest people.

SHIRLEY

Don't do that, I'll catch the wasps in jars and let them go outside.

BILL

You're barmy! Just kill them before they kill you!

*Fade out.*

## Scene 4

BILL *is in the house.* SHIRLEY *walks in through the front door.*

BILL

You're late. It's hell in here. They're still here. Not as bad as it was half an hour ago though. Sounded like a jet engine. I've got to get out. It's making me sick. You said you'd deal with it. Don't know why I listened. I'm ringing the exterminator now.

SHIRLEY

Oh . . . that's strange. I caught them all, one by one . . . in a jar, and let them go. They understood and didn't sting me. They assured me it was all right, they were just cold and scared. We don't want to hurt them, Bill . . . and that poison the exterminator uses won't be good for the twins.

BILL

Would you prefer they got stung?

SHIRLEY

No, of course not. [*She looks confused and upset.*] Well, I guess you'd better ring. Not all of those wasps are happy, I guess I should admit it. Yes, you'd better ring. There could be trouble.

BILL

You mean a catastrophe!

SHIRLEY

I even blocked the cracks and holes. I can't understand how they're getting in.

BILL

Don't tell me they've spontaneously generated out of thin air. I'm sure that's coming next.

SHIRLEY

Let's open the windows.

BILL

Don't open the windows! I tried that and their numbers doubled. Huge numbers have been clustering outside the windows, communicating through the glass to those trapped inside. Those in want out, and those out want in.

I'm confused, Bill!

Come on, Shirley. How I haven't been stung yet, I don't know. I've had them in my hair, buzzing my face, caught in the filaments of my jumper. Listen to them, just listen to them. They eat into your brain.

[*They start to duck and weave, attempting to avoid the wasps. Hypnotic music should be played. They dance so they constantly cross each other's paths in chasing wasps, but stylistically avoid physical contact. It should be coldly intimate. If possible, a huge spiral image (trance disk) should be revolving in the background, mesmerising the audience. This ritualistic play within the play should go on for about four or five minutes. The lighting should be "psychedelic", then "white light" when they eventually exclaim. Music stops suddenly.*]

[*Together.*] They have gone! We are alone and it is quiet . . .

*Blackout.*

# Act 2

## Scene 1

*Bedroom.* SHIRLEY *and* BILL *preparing for bed.*

SHIRLEY

Why do you go on about it all the time?

BILL

I don't go on about it all the time. [*He sneezes.*] There, look, I'm sick.

SHIRLEY

Sorry, Bill . . . I just feel tense when the twins are away. And things aren't right in the house at the moment. The scratching is getting louder, and I can hear that buzzing sound.

BILL

I can't hear anything. I think they've gone. Maybe the cold has killed them off. Glad we didn't get the exterminator in after all. Saved at least a hundred quid. How about a cuddle then, I need reassurance.

SHIRLEY

Sure, cuddles are free!

BILL

Thanks, Shirley. Sorry, I'm actually feeling stressed as well. Not just the wasps. It didn't go well at work today. Haven't had a chance to unload it. The Ambassador is blaming me about the confusion over the safety policy.

SHIRLEY

[Coming from her side of the bed to cuddle him.] Oh Bill, don't worry, think positive. If you're positive it will work out. Take a few deep breaths and clear your mind. Jump into bed and I'll rub your back with some essential oils.

*They break apart and* SHIRLEY *goes to the other side of the bed and takes a couple of small bottles from the drawer, briefly consults her crystals, and climbs in.* BILL *shakes his hands, takes deep breaths, then pulls off his jeans and lowers himself into bed before erupting in a scream.*

BILL

Shit! Ouch!! Shit, what the hell is that? [*He leaps out of bed and grabs his leg.* SHIRLEY *leaps out and rips back the covers.*]

SHIRLEY

It's a wasp. [*She scrapes it off the bed and into a jar as* BILL *falls to the floor, clutching his leg.*]

BILL

I'm in pain, Shirley. I'm in real pain! I've been poisoned. It's burning me up inside! I feel like I'm going to pass out. The pain is excruciating!

SHIRLEY

[*Studying the wasp closely.*] This is your anger and frustration, Bill. It's the darkness coming through. Remember what it says in the Old Testament.

BILL

What does it say? I don't care what it says! Have some pity, Shirley!

*Blackout.*

## Scene 2

*Morning. Breakfast.*

BILL

[*Looking seedy and holding his injured leg out.*] I've called them.

SHIRLEY

I still don't think it's necessary. We should handle the problem ourselves. That was probably the last one, Bill.

BILL

I can hear that buzzing again and there was scratching in the ceiling over our bed all night long. It's not easy to sleep with your leg swollen like this. It could just have easily been you, and with your allergy . . . I dreamt it again, Shirley. I'm worried about you. You never have check-ups. Your eyes have changed colour lately. They've gone from blue to a murky grey. I think I caught my illness off you. For both our sakes, you should see someone about it.

SHIRLEY

It wouldn't have stung me. None of them will. I know. And I feel perfectly healthy. You're just a little upset. When the leg settles down you'll be fine.

BILL

Shirley, I can't cope with this much longer. If you don't want to think of me, think of the kids. They'll be frightened.

SHIRLEY

[*Again shaken.*] Yes, that's true. What time will they be here?

BILL

Nine.

SHIRLEY

I've got to work today, you know that.

BILL

You'll have to call in sick?

SHIRLEY

Can't you? You've got the poisoned leg. You shouldn't be going to work. I am reading cards at lunch.

BILL

It's not so bad now, that blue stuff helped a little. And I've got to be at work or the Ambassador will be after my blood. I have to be there no matter how ill I am. You know what the Old Man's like!

SHIRLEY

[Aside.] My grandmother's remedy. She applied it to mine, though it didn't help. [Focussing.] Why do you run after that monster so hard?

BILL

That's my job. [Pause.] I don't like having people in the house without one of us being here.

Fade out.

## Scene 3

Knock at the door. SHIRLEY answers. STAN enters looking like something from a toxic zone, or a biological testing lab, or an astronaut. He has the evangeliser about him, and can become quite menacing. He stands close to those he is talking to.

SHIRLEY

Come in.

STAN

[Without a hello.] Been looking around outside – wasps around the windows, along the guttering. They'll be in the roof.

[155]

#### SHIRLEY

Hello . . . yes, above the ceiling. Been a lot of noise up there. We blocked the various cracks and holes we could find, but more wasps are coming in this morning. And my husband was stung last night.

#### STAN

So Amanda told me. That's my girlfriend, she works in reception.

#### SHIRLEY

[*Ignoring him.*] Oh. There must be entry points we can't see.

#### STAN

Always is in these old places. [*He pokes about, surveys the place.*] Looks pretty modern inside though. Looks can be deceiving.

#### SHIRLEY

Yes, my husband likes things clean. He doesn't like the smell of age, doesn't like grime.

#### STAN

Seems strange to live in such an old place then. You could sell this and move into a place near Canary Wharf, or into one of those new apartments perched over the river.

#### SHIRLEY

He says that if you live in London you've got to be seen to appreciate history. It's to do with his work. With entertaining.

#### STAN

Ah, the best of both worlds, eh. Having his cake and eating it too. Australians? The new world meets the old.

#### SHIRLEY

[*Slightly flustered.*] Something like that. [*Changing the subject.*] How long will it take? I'm not happy about this but if we don't get it done it'll cause problems for the children, and my husband. They don't bother me, even though I'm allergic.

STAN

[*Very close.*] A few hours; then you'll have to be out of the place for a few hours more. Actually, best if you leave now.

SHIRLEY

I can't.

STAN

You should, it'll get toxic.

SHIRLEY

I'll move to the opposite end of the flat, then move back again as you work your way up or do whatever it is you do.

STAN

Well, I shouldn't treat the place if you're going to stay inside.

SHIRLEY

Tell you what, I'll read on the balcony – it's another warm day.

STAN

Okay. I'll put chemical down in the roof first. [*He mutters something to himself, maybe a scripture.*] Lot of magic stuff in here. Are you a believer?

SHIRLEY

Oh, I'm just an amateur. I read cards, palms, use aromatic oils. That kind of thing.

STAN

Can be a dangerous thing messing with the other side.

SHIRLEY

Oh, I'm always respectful. I don't mess with the dark stuff.

STAN

[*Hesitating, studying her closely.*] You don't say. Well, that's good. It's powerful. [*He starts to poke around, as if looking for holes, cracks.*] Can't see any wasps . . .

SHIRLEY

Oh, I hoovered them up, swept them out, caught them in a jar.


STAN

Don't like having to kill them. Admirable creatures really. Social beings. I don't like killing anything. I admire ants, rats, all highly advanced species. But sometimes it's got to be done. [*He looks at her and laughs bizarrely.*] I suppose you could say that I'm a form of exorcist. I work with God to mop up the plagues he's sent, when he's decided that the damage inflicted has been adequate.


SHIRLEY

[*Almost terrified.*] I'll go outside now and leave you to it.


STAN

Might get you to read my cards before I go. You know, just by way of fun.


*He disappears.* SHIRLEY *goes to the balcony and starts reading. She's obviously uncomfortable and waves her hands around her face.*


SHIRLEY

Wasps. It's impossible out here. If I switch my mind to my book they'll go elsewhere. [*She concentrates.*] They are so loud . . .


STAN *opens the door to the balcony, ducking as he does so.*


STAN

Whoops, let a few more in. Won't make any difference, though. It's the biggest wasps' nest I have ever seen. I'll have to write about this one. I write about these things, you know. I don't like killing anything, so I write about things.


SHIRLEY

How does that stop the killing?

STAN

Helps the scientists find new ways of tackling the problem. Exorcism shouldn't be messy. Should be a case of silent running.

SHIRLEY

Can you fix it?

STAN

Yes, but I'll have to drill holes through your bedroom ceiling to apply the chemical. That's where they're concentrated.

SHIRLEY

It's so disgusting. It's just disgusting. [*She checks herself.*] Sorry, I'm beginning to sound like my husband!

STAN

I understand how you feel. There's a language for it. Violated, intruded upon, polluted. In a city like this, you call it fate. [*Pause.*] I can comfort you if you like . . .

SHIRLEY

What?!

STAN

I mean, say a few comforting words. Or maybe you can say some to me before I begin. It's a big job. I wouldn't say no to a cup of tea before I get started. Maybe it's an opportune time to read my cards – might prevent me making a mistake.

SHIRLEY

They are inside, I'll get them.

*She disappears and* STAN *stretches, rubbing his chest, adjusting his crotch.*

STAN

[*To himself.*] No telling what kind of day it's going to turn out to be. But spring is surely in the air. Nice to hear the blackbirds – they've a lovely garden.

#### SHIRLEY

[*Back with cards.*] Take a seat. [*She proceeds to read his cards. This is done silently until the last card is revealed.*] I have never seen such lucky cards.

#### STAN

Oh, it doesn't surprise me. I make my own luck. Some of my colleagues have been sick from using the chemicals, but I haven't missed a day. They say it's there in the fat, but I keep trim.

#### SHIRLEY

[*Drops the cards,* STAN *picks them up. The last one he places upright on the table.*] Death!

#### STAN

Death to the wasps. I'm off to get started. I appreciate the trust you place in me by letting me into your house. Your private space. Into your bedroom. Don't feel bad about it. We learn decorum in the trade, and confidentiality is the name of the game. And if there are any ongoing problems I'll be round in a flash. I'll leave you my mobile number when I go. Don't hesitate to call. We are, I am . . . . thorough.

#### SHIRLEY

I'll be out on the balcony . . . if you need me.

#### STAN

I'll start the treatment, then give you a call when I've finished. Don't forget, it's a good idea to leave the house empty for a few hours. The fumes are deadly.

*Psychedelic or trance music intensifies, colours swirl. A bad trip.*

*Fade out.*

# Scene 4

*In the loungeroom.*

**BILL**

[*On the phone.*] Yes Mum, it's like a horror scene here. The twins are back tomorrow and the house is infested. I've got to get out. And I've been unwell and I'm worried about Shirley . . . Well, she's been odd lately . . . Yes, odder than usual, Mum! I mean unwell . . . She thinks she's in fine fettle but I can tell, I can see there's something very wrong . . . No, no . . . well, I don't know. Women's trouble . . . . I don't know, Mum. You think there's something she's not telling me . . . ? Might be so . . . She's sick and doesn't know it. The exterminator drilled dozens of holes in the ceiling, filled the roof with poison, and patched them up with plaster that showered over the bed. He's ruined the doona you gave us for Christmas, and driven thousands of wasps into the house through God knows what points of entry. Shirley is waiting outside for the idiot to appear now. Yes, yes . . . I've got to go to work. Will give you a call. Sometimes I just want to pack up and come home.

**SHIRLEY**

[*Enters through the open front door, ducking to evade wasp.* BILL *mutters something further on the phone and quickly hangs up.*] Who was on the phone?

**BILL**

Just Mum.

**SHIRLEY**

What time is it down there? Must be very late?

**BILL**

Yes, she's got insomnia. You know how she gets.

**SHIRLEY**

She should take that Sleepy Tea I told her about.

BILL

She doesn't like that kooky hippy stuff.

SHIRLEY

The exterminator will be here shortly. Don't be angry with him, it's a tough job. The toughest he's ever had. He says it will become a legend among exterminators. I shouldn't really call him that, he doesn't like it.

BILL

So he's got delicate feelings, has he? Ridiculous. I've had to take two valium today. Things with the Ambassador won't be any easier. How can I explain to him that I spent the night barricaded in the lounge-room, with mosquito nets the only thing between us and total annihilation? It's like the plagues of Egypt. A circle of Hell.

SHIRLEY

Just go to work dear, I'll look after it. [*She's eager to get rid of him but he's too neurotic to pick it up.*]

BILL

Yes, I'm out of here. Sorry to leave you with it again. I'll make it up to you . . .

SHIRLEY

It's okay, darling, just go and look after the Ambassador.

BILL *exits.*

STAN

[*Poking his head round.*] World War 3, I hear. Your hubby was pretty upset, our Amanda tells me.

SHIRLEY

With good reason.

STAN

Now, keep calm. It's the only way to handle situations like this.

SHIRLEY

[*Almost flirting.*] Would you like your cards done before you begin?

STAN

[*Flattered.*] Have to be out on the balcony, there are too many wasps in here. It's getting dangerous! [*They laugh.*]

*They move on to the balcony.*

STAN

Beautiful day. I love this garden.

SHIRLEY

Won't be long before I start working up the herb garden. I grow all sorts of herbs – healing herbs mainly.

STAN

[*Jokingly.*] Amanda's pretty angry with me at the moment, says she shouldn't have to clean up after me – your hubby gave her a real basting. Do you grow anything for troubled love-lives?

SHIRLEY

[*Embarrassed.*] That's a trade secret. No, let's check the cards. [*They repeat the process.*] I can't believe it, EXACTLY the same configuration. Nothing has changed. That's impossible.

STAN

Don't you believe in your own cards?

SHIRLEY

I do, I . . . [*She stands up and walks to the edge of the balcony.* STAN *moves up close behind her, his toxic suit pressed against her back. Music starts.*] Stop it! Get off me!

STAN

Sorry, I was just trying to comfort you. It's good to release tension.

SHIRLEY

Please don't crowd me, I don't like people being so close to me. Please move away.

*He does. The music intensifies.*

SHIRLEY

I can't stand the sound of those wasps. Please, please kill them. Kill them all!

STAN

[*He looks excited, thrilled.*] Sorry, didn't mean to crowd. Why do you wear such stuffy clothing? You've got plenty of nice delicate stuff. Sorry, but I can't help noticing when I do a job. Have you ever thought what it must feel like to die? To die in your sleep, or to be hit by a car, or to be poisoned? This is arsenic-based poison. It's a horrible death. I've been researching the wasps' nervous system. Do you know that strychnine makes a human hallucinate? [*He almost wraps himself around her.*]

SHIRLEY

[*Releasing a small scream and ducking away.*] Just fix the problem!

STAN

Don't mince words, you want me to exterminate. That's the role you have in mind for me. Okay then, it's the death card. I will kill them, I'll kill them all!!

*He dances into and then around the apartment exterminating unseen wasps. It is a sexualised ritualistic act that mimics the original dance. Finished, he calls* SHIRLEY *who is outside.*

STAN

I have cleansed your home. You must keep out for three hours. Just time to rush through and out into the day. [*He starts to chant.*]

These are European Wasps,
as you're probably aware.
Why do you care where

they come from? You just
want them gone.

*[Chants back. The pace increases. Another dance begins, working towards a
frenzy.]*

I feared the European
Kodachrome, intravenous
totems and savages
in steel boats, tinfoil planes,
a teenager,
it had just arrived
and swarms
might separate us,
parties making politics
out of fear
drummed-up
on maps and schematics,
struggling as the multiple stings
flowed down into blood: the warnings
were slow in coming
but shocked us
when they did:
the immolation,
the sticky stuff
that's the medium . . .

STAN
Don't underestimate
the English wasp, close
kin to the European,
its markings much the same.
The currency of the Europeans
warrants the title Killer,
even though it's only a rumour.

SHIRLEY

Hexagonally chambered
sickly sweet as pheromones
in char houses and crypts,
metal-brittle legs wheedling
and coercing,
like pubic hairs
floating around the plughole,
I hate strangers
in my bathroom;
architectural tiers,
committees dishing out
the money, a class,
a gridwork of geometric ownership,
they feed the pigs on plenty;
one egg per cell,
a paper lithographed,
font and leading
like the Venice of Italy
before unification
as saliva mixes
to pulp materials
affecting vowels
like colourants:
carcinogenic consonants
leaving no room
for manoeuvre.


STAN

Have you danced the tarantella?


SHIRLEY

My husband fell to the floor
after being stung by a wasp,
I wanted to lift him to dance
as if stung by the Apulian Spider
as if all poisons would force us
into a frenzy, or the call of Saint Vitus

would obscure and remake
his virility, where no thirst
no hunger no end to the dance
would relieve him.

                              STAN
Dancing like that, a girl lost an arm . . .

                                    SHIRLEY
Native wasp
larvae consumes
spiders, cicadas, other insects;
I plot a spider paralysed,
cryogenic mother
inlaying biology
to lay the larvae,
to say trapdoors and huntsmans
pacified in mud huts
as adults process
flightplans, feed
on nectar gathered
electrically, poisoned poisoned
the memory stimulated
by death, exorcism!

STAN *and* SHIRLEY *lock together and* . . .

*Blackout.*

# Act 3

*A new house. Entirely modern. No signs of New Age, magic paraphernalia. On the Thames.*

## Scene 1

#### BILL

Haven't touched your cards this evening. Something wrong?

#### SHIRLEY

[*Flat.*] It's the place, it's dead.

#### BILL

You haven't given it a chance yet. I love it, it's so clean. [*A little nervous.*] And wasp-free! And rat-free. I feel good for the first time in ages! Though I do worry about mosquitoes from the Thames during summer. I think we should have that balcony decking closed in – would be good for plants in winter.

#### SHIRLEY

[*Sullen, closed-off.*] It's just pointless. The girls at work have said I'm losing my spark. I don't feel at my best.

#### BILL

They had no choice but move us out of there, the place was a toxic waste dump. For a guy who reckons he didn't like killing he really went overboard. I tell you, you should get a check-up. Your eyes look awful.

#### SHIRLEY

I dreamt last night that I was killed by wasps.

BILL

No, they've gone. Don't worry. [*He sneezes and looks surprised.*] Oh, God, don't tell me I'm getting it again. Never a break.

SHIRLEY

[*Distracted.*] The exterminator has ingested and absorbed neuro-poisons for years. He says they heighten his awareness. Allow him to make contact. He spoke to the house and it told him that it wanted to be free. He told me to let go.

*Long pause. Music lifts and drops, lights swirl.*

BILL

[*Listening.*] Funny, thought I heard a buzzing sound. [*To himself, trying to work it out.*] Post-traumatic shock, maybe. I got like this as a kid once when I saw a traffic accident on the corner just down from home. I could hear the crunching sound every night as I went to bed. Lasted for months. It was so vivid!

[*He picks at his jumper. And begins again almost absent-mindedly.*] I remember as a kid watching them pour chemicals on the housepads as the neighbourhood grew and the bush lots were bulldozed. They drenched the yellow sand with spray before laying concrete slabs. I wondered why the concrete slabs didn't slide off.

SHIRLEY

The twins don't like it here. They'll never recover from this – arriving back to hear they're living somewhere else.

BILL

They'll get used to it. [*Starts looking around the room, listening hard . . .*] Listen! Listen . . . Can you hear it?

SHIRLEY

I can't hear anything. Maybe the river if I listen hard.

BILL

It's a wasp.

SHIRLEY

The river. You're just not used to it being so close.

BILL

I know the sound of a wasp when I hear one. We must have brought some live ones over – caught up in our clothes, in the kids' toys. There were so many corpses among the toys . . . Maybe we missed a live one. Maybe it was a queen! [*He starts getting hysterical.*] I can't believe it, I can hear more than one. I can hear them.

SHIRLEY

You're just being paranoid. Calm down. It's nothing. This place is dead, spiritless.

BILL

We've been afflicted!

SHIRLEY

Bill, get a grip. This is ridiculous. [*She walks around the room, examining the contents and walls.*] There's nothing here. It's only the river, and any spirit that had was extracted when they cleaned up the pollution.

BILL

[*As if enlightened.*] No, Shirley, you're wrong. That's it. They're coming out of the river. That's where they come from. I used to catch them as a kid, did I ever tell you that? It's punishment. Punishment.

[*He starts to dance and chant, working into a frenzy . . .* ]

Striking deep into the crisp
salvers of dead jasmine flowers
the paper wasp outpaces
the eye —
the elapsed witherings
of its avionics,
high pitched and devastating.

The nest of a paper wasp – thin grey
parchment chambers
moving towards opacity
bloom from a common
point, anchored stiffly
against the scent
of jasmine.

The wasp is the part
of a nest that flies.
Its wings the harp
on which frenzied
lullabies are cut.

[SHIRLEY *tries to hold him, and gets caught up in the dance, but constantly
trying to stop him as she participates. He gets louder as he "recites".*]

A tiger with yellow stripes
would prefer to remain still
amongst the foliage,
watch as you pass confidently
by.
    As evening settles
like a fusty blanket, summer
heat pricking even the space
between carapace and skin,
the wasps move slowly
over the nest's chambers.
Even the full moon
lifting its yellow eye
over the rim of the fence
can revitalize them.
The pull of the sun
cannot be mimicked.

                    SHIRLEY
Bill, Bill, you are scaring me! Please stop this!

*[He pushes her away and leans against the wall, reciting the following lines in a calmer but breathless voice.]*

To separate a wasp's nest
from the jasmine – fierce
undertaking I should refuse,
but wishing to preserve
both it and my child's
inquisitive
and vulnerable flesh,
I seek merely
to transfer
to a place
safer for both.
Two wasps
and a nest
in a coffee jar:
an impression
in the moon's
limp light.

Moisture
from night waterings
lifts the lawns
and gardens
in the early morning.
Wasps' fire
in the coffee jar,
their nest precarious
on its glass floor,
holdfast swimming
the petrified current.

SHIRLEY

If you don't stop Bill, STOP, Stop it. You'll wake the twins. There's nothing here. There's nothing here at all. It's a dead place . . .

[*Lunging for* SHIRLEY.] Get out of my head, Shirley, get out! [*He grabs at her neck but she jumps aside and he falls onto the corner of a table, and then "dead" to the ground.*]

*The light changes from "white" to red. Music intensifies. Frenzied.*

*Blackout.*

## Scene 2

*A few days later.* STAN *is talking to* SHIRLEY *in the living room.*

SHIRLEY

He insists that you check the place.

STAN

Strange for a man who wants to sue me.

SHIRLEY

There's no explaining it. He's in the bedroom – stay out of there. Been in bed for days now. Keeps yelling out, hallucinating. Thinks he's back in Australia looking for paper wasp nests. Just check the place over. There's nothing here, he's just upset. The doctor was here last night and he says it's a minor breakdown. Took some blood samples and sedated him. Gently.

STAN

[*Looking about, menacing.*] No time for the cards today?

SHIRLEY

[*Nervously, but still in control.*] No, no time for cards. I've given them away.

STAN

Ah, lost your calling? I see a lot of that in my line of work. Did wonders for my love-life. Amanda and I are really firing.

SHIRLEY

I'm pleased for you.

STAN

[*Abruptly.*] Well, nothing here. Should I check the bedroom?

SHIRLEY

That's not a good idea.

STAN

But he obviously wanted me here.

SHIRLEY

But not in there.

STAN

[*Moving very close.*] That's where the wasps will be, you know that.

*A long pause.*

SHIRLEY

Yes, possibly . . . I don't know, you should go now.

STAN

[*Threatening but sickly sweet.*] You'll just have to face up to it, I'll need to treat the room. You know that's where they are. You're in denial. You've heard them.

SHIRLEY

[*Upset.*] No, I don't hear them. There's nothing here, it's a dead place! He's so strange at the moment. He scares the twins. I had so much trouble getting them off to school, this morning. They're confused. He sees things, he sees giant wasps crawling down the walls, over the beds. And they bite him, they bite him so hard he sees colours, and feels the poison burning through his body. It makes him monstrous and twisted. I can't sleep in there any longer.

STAN

He tries to do things to you?

SHIRLEY

Yes.

STAN

Strange things? Out of character?

SHIRLEY

Yes. Leave it alone. Go now, just go.

*Noise in the background . . .*

BILL

[*Offstage, screaming.*] Help! They're all over me, they're stinging me. They are eating me! [*The following lines should boom through the theatre.*]

Lightning gravitates
between ground
& thunderhead:
the dark bodies
of wasps almost
neon-charged
by thunderbolts.
The paper bell tolls
& wings flick
like static & then as the dark
silence between flashes
smothers the nest
they slip into stasis.
Again & again—
like a faulty power point—
they throw out
the occasional blue spark

& then, as the storm passes
& humidity gives way
to a cool change
they lose
their spark.
Winter approaches.
The nest diminishes
& we forget to make daily observations.
They wait, their spirits
feeding the Queen. Couriers
to the other side!

*A brilliant rush of white light – blinding. Then blackout.*

## Scene 3

*Funeral. Morbid music.*

STAN

I'm glad I can be here for you at a time like this.

SHIRLEY

He should have been buried in Australia. The Embassy wouldn't cover
it. The soil's all wrong here. The clay clings to the spade. It is never
dry down that deep. He will always be sodden.

STAN

But everyone is so calm, and so respectful.

SHIRLEY

It was nice of Amanda to read the eulogy poems at the service.

STAN

Yes, that was nice. She says she feels she knew him better than anyone
else.

**SHIRLEY**

I sprinkled some eucalypt oil over the casket.

**STAN**

It was a beautiful service.

**SHIRLEY**

I looked up wasps in the library and learnt a lot more. They specialise in loopholes. I believe the toxicity levels in his blood were just a smoke screen, it was purely psychological.

**STAN**

The Gospels will bring comfort where the cards failed.

**SHIRLEY**

The local church has been very supportive. The twins are thriving. I realise how closed off they were from the world.

It is time to dig
the memory's fertile beds,
catch the raucous bird
& hope for a break
in the weather,
to observe the single cell
of a queen expand
into a bell, its cells
holding the first group
of workers.

**STAN**

You see, if we'd killed the queen straight out things would have been different. But there was probably more than one queen.

**SHIRLEY**

I've read that they assert themselves in warm weather, and wither in the cold. Though in the warmth of the ceiling, a queen might persist, and new queens colonise nearby, connecting into super-cities of death. In Australia they drive out the native wasps. I am allergic. I suffer anaphylaxis. Nothing will change that, even the cold compress of ice and snow. My blood is too hot.

STAN

Vespula Germanica. That's the European wasp.

SHIRLEY

The river sounds so pleasant at night. A subdued hum. It's like a warm current running through my body. I feel at peace.

> The wasps are slow now,
> the last batch of workers
> crawls slowly over
> the uncapped cells.
> I record my observations.
> Soon I shall retire
> from this season of evolution
> & extinction . . .

STAN

After a while one becomes acclimatised to the poison. I'm sure the old house will take you back – you and the twins. I read it in your cards.

*They begin to dance. Gentle medieval music then segues into "Interstellar Overdrive" Pink Floyd or DJ Spooky track. A death dance that reaches Bacchic trance-fury before rapid collapse. Spotlight burning to a narrow point then blackout, silence.*

THE END

# Paydirt

*An Unperformable Play in Six Disintegrating Acts*

## Characters

*The "secondary" players can be doubled, even tripled. Other than two or three of these players, characters may be more ciphers than "real" people.*

SAMUEL

WILLIAM

BELINDA

JULIA

ZOË

REG

JOE

BENNY

BARMAN

BARMAID

2 POLICEMEN

CAB DRIVER

# The set

The play is set in an inner-city hotel and its immediate surroundings. The real focus of the play is SAMUEL, and his journey of visionary decline. Though there is little narrative action, there should be significant shifts in the audience's perception of SAMUEL's decay. In essence, SAMUEL is reconstructing years of wandering and denial through his interactions with a group of fellow drinkers and drug-users over one day. These are hardened drinkers, so drunkenness comes and goes. The play is not a presentation of outrageous behaviours associated with addiction: addiction is to be used as a metaphor for various internal struggles. There are strong elements of The Odyssey in here, though the voyage has already been made, and the return long since "celebrated". This is the dross, the residue. Lighting is vital to the piece, as is music. The bar is not simply a darkly-lit place, but a tableau on to which primary colours are washed, with darkness edging in. Some lights are too bright and need to be quelled – slashes of lighting against the backdrop. In some ways, SAMUEL's morphic fadeout in the end is a scene of perverse rapture. This is a miracle play in which the miracle is hard to spot. Other characters come in and out of focus, and thus it is essential some doubling – at least – take place. They are really the same people. Is SAMUEL really married to BELINDA, or is it a "game" being played out of social "conventions" the uninitiated are not privy to? Music is a mixture of jukebox rock, and more ritualistic rhythms. The combination and movement of these is essential. Clear moments of burlesque – the dance of the policemen, their dressing in drag – should be juxtaposed with the momentary majesty of the other characters. The burlesque is intended to highlight the depravity of "law" in this place. The cabaret scenes are intended to be over the top – death and dissolution break all inhibitions, in a way that mere drunkenness cannot. These are moments of celebration of the miracle, the miracle of having seen. SAMUEL has seen, and to some extent towards the end, understood.

# Act 1

## Scene 1

*Scene: Hotel public bar. Set in an L shape with a few tables and chairs, a pool table. In one of the corners, probably the one furthest away from the exit marked "toilets", sits a jukebox. The hotel bar, just opened – it is just after sunrise. Two men in their late twenties or early thirties enter, following the barman. Neither has slept though both are in high spirits and sarcastic as always.*

SAMUEL

I love this place at times like this.

WILLIAM

I'm not so sure.

SAMUEL

What d'you reckon, Mr. Barman? Good place for losers? For those who seek to trip the light fantastic and come a cropper? In the Kingdom of the Blind, the one-eyed man is king! In the Williams pub a whole shearing team of one-eyed men chased me out of the public bar and into the car park. I climbed the roof. They had me trapped there, but I outwitted them.

BARMAN

I wouldn't know about that, gents. What do you want?

SAMUEL

I'm for a triple tequila – ha, sunrise. Yes, I slid back down into the courtyard and hid under the tables stacked up against a wall. They climbed that roof and thought I'd vanished into thin air. One fell and broke his neck. By that time, I was out of there.

BARMAN

Williams? Isn't that on the road to Albany?

SAMUEL

Sure is. [*He meditates briefly.*] Albany – ex-whaling community. They slaughtered the Leviathan. Grabbed it by the short and curlies. Speared the beasts with explosive harpoons. The seas get rough down there. It's not unusual for King Waves – freak waves they call them – to reach right up and grab someone standing on a rock, even a cliff. It's the Leviathan calling. [*He meditates briefly again.*] Whales have never struck me as being vengeful creatures though. Not really their way.

BARMAN

You going to drink your drink?

SAMUEL

Certainly, certainly. Gotta drink your drink when it's handed to you. I wouldn't want to be different now, would I? That way I end up in trouble. Okay, William – a beer or a tequila?

WILLIAM

A beer.

*There is a silence as their drinks are served. Both men swivel on bar stools and eye the place over.*

SAMUEL

Mind if I play the jukebox?

BARMAN

No problem.

SAMUEL

[*Walks over, sees it turned off.*] Power?

BARMAN

Okay.

SAMUEL

[*Examines playlist.*] Hey, William, check out the arrangement. It's prehistoric. Great. Look, we can listen to Led Zeppelin, T-Rex . . . the list goes on.

*He places some money in the jukebox. Throughout the play, references will be made to the music, but the audience will never hear it. Only the players are party to it.*

SAMUEL

[*Pulling out a $100 bill.*] Another drink, please . . . [*Looks at* WILLIAM.]

WILLIAM

Not yet, thanks. You're flush . . .

*Enter* JULIA, ZOË, *and* BENNY.

JULIA *is wearing a low-slung black dress and suspenders.* ZOË *is dressed in men's clothes a few sizes too large for her.* BENNY *is slickly attired in white denim, sunglasses, a hat. They break off in the centre of the stage –* BENNY *goes to the bar. Meanwhile* SAMUEL *has wandered over to the pool table and is bouncing the white ball off cushions, aiming for a pocket after three or four rebounds.*

SAMUEL

[*To* WILLIAM.] Feel like a game?

WILLIAM

Yeah, why not.

SAMUEL *sets the game up.* WILLIAM *wanders over, saying "hi" to the women as he passes.* JULIA *replies likewise.* ZOË *ignores him.* BENNY, *having purchased the beer, sits at the women's table.* ZOË *does not drink.*

SAMUEL

Mind if I break?

WILLIAM

Na . . .

SAMUEL

[*Glint in his eye.*] You wanted to say "mugs away".

WILLIAM

[*Laughing generously.*] Maybe.

SAMUEL

[*Bends.*] Nothing down.

*Suddenly the stage goes dark with the exception of "sunlight" filtering through the cracks of the "front"door. When the lights come back on,* SAMUEL *is sitting next to* JULIA *and* ZOË, *while* BENNY *is playing pool with* WILLIAM.

BARMAN

Sorry about that, folks. [*Pause.*] A fuse.

*Those at the table look at each other and then burst into laughter.*

ZOË

That bloke wouldn't know . . . [*She laughs and leaves it hanging.*]

SAMUEL

[*To* JULIA.] So you'd like a tequila, eh. OK. Everyone should have a tequila. After all, we're under the volcano, aren't we?

*The joke falls flat and* SAMUEL *reasserts himself by pulling a $100 note from his pocket.*

SAMUEL

Right, what will it be: single, double, triple, quad?

JULIA

Quad. [*She reaches for her bag.*] I'll get it.

SAMUEL

[*Removing her hand.*] No, no – it's okay. I'll get it. After all, it's the only exercise I've been getting lately.

JULIA *and* ZOË *laugh sarcastically.*

SAMUEL

[*From the bar – he's forgotten the order.*] Now, what was it? Ah, that's right . . .

*He orders and returns, balancing drinks, and sits between them.* JULIA *moves closer to him.*

JULIA

Haven't seen you for a while.

SAMUEL

Nor me you. Back on the game?

JULIA

Yeah. For a little bit.

SAMUEL

[*Laughing.*] Still forty dollars for a head job?

ZOË

[*Laughing.*] She can't do no more, she's full up.

JULIA

[*Slowly – as if she's somewhere else.*] Just room enough for one more . . .

SAMUEL

Well, if you're looking at me you might as well enjoy your tequila because that's about all you'd get out of me this morning.

Hey, Samuel. Benny here wants to know if you've got a spare smoke.

SAMUEL *tosses him a packet of rollie tobacco.*

SAMUEL

Give that to him.

WILLIAM

Thanks. I might take you up on that beer now.

SAMUEL

Yeah, well, you can get it. And another triple for me. Got a thirst this morning. Just slammin' it down. [*He pauses, reflects.*] Just slammin' it down . . .

WILLIAM *walks over, reaches into* SAMUEL*'s top pocket and takes the money.* SAMUEL *grabs him round the legs and hugs him.* WILLIAM *goes to the bar.*

## Scene 2

*An hour later. Bar is busy.* REG *and* JOE *are angry with* JULIA.

REG

I don't give a fuck, you bitch. You said you'd meet me last night and you didn't turn up.

JULIA

That's what you say. And anyway I wouldn't let either of you creeps touch me.

BENNY *wanders over, sits down.* REG *and* JOE *mutter, look at each other, and head for the bar.* SAMUEL *enters from the toilet.*

JULIA

Where the fuck were you when needed, eh?

SAMUEL

Dead.

JULIA

Yeah, I can believe it.

ZOË *laughs nervously.*

SAMUEL

Well, what happened?

JULIA

Don't worry about it.

*A long silence.*

SAMUEL

It's strange, you know. Whenever I walk through that door [*points to toilets*] I somehow feel I no longer have any relevance.

JULIA

[*Snidely.*] Don't worry, dear. When any of us walk through that door we feel something. In my case it's usually an ache somewhere in the region of the bladder.

SAMUEL

Top answer. Tops. Drinks?

*Hands* ZOË *money. She goes to the bar.*

JULIA

You're right, you know. I mean, I understand you. I reckon I'm the only one here that understands you. Oh, and William, but he's different. I reckon you mean that when you've been with people and you suddenly leave them everything falls out of place.

ZOË

Sounds like it's getting ruder.

[*Playfully hits* ZOË.] Fuck you, bitch.

*They all laugh.*

TWO POLICEMEN *enter, look around, walk to the bar and have a quiet word with the* BARMAN. *After a moment's silence everybody begins talking again. It is as if they almost will the policemen out again – who, though hesitating at the door, do not look back again.*

## Scene 3

ZOË'S *story.*

ZOË

[*To* SAMUEL.] You got enough money for a packet-a-chips? I'm hungry.

SAMUEL

Sure. [*Hands it to her. She goes to get up but he grabs her arm.*] Hey, Julia says you've got to be in court at ten o'clock.

ZOË

I'm not gonna go today.

SAMUEL

You'd better.

ZOË

Nah, the magistrate that's on today hates blackfellas.

SAMUEL

The cops have already seen you here. They know you. They'll just walk straight down and pick you up.

ZOË

Nah, not today. Besides, they're afraid I'll bite them. Yah know – AIDS, the pox. [*She laughs and goes for her chips.*]

SAMUEL

[*Yelling out across the room to her.*] Get me a tequila.

ZOË

[*Without turning around.*] Get it yourself, you smart white bastard.

SAMUEL

Hey, what's that for. I'm your mate.

ZOË

Yeah, thanks, mate.

SAMUEL

Fuck it. Hey, William, leave that fuckin' pool table and come and talk to me.

WILLIAM

Not now, Samuel, I'm on the black. It's my game . . .

SAMUEL

Smart arse. [*Agitated.*] I want to tell you about my journey across town getting here at the crack of dawn this morning, Julia. I want to tell you how the cab I was in narrowly missed being crushed between a cop car and the sparkling white Commodore V8 it was chasing. The kids driving the Commodore jumped the traffic island and came straight at us, the cab swerved, the kids lost it, spun, and the cops slammed straight into the passenger's side, killing a young girl. The cab driver rang triple O and we checked out the wreckage. Only the girl was dead. Broke her neck. She wasn't really cut much. The driver ran, and the cops – not a scratch on them – went after him and left the dead girl strapped in her seat. Nothing much else to be said. The ambulance came, and more cops, and they took statements, and eventually we got on our way, the traffic backed for miles. It was clear sailing moving forward – the rough seas were behind us.

JULIA

[*Uncomfortable.*] Fucking pigs. Are you okay? You're a bit lost now, aren't you?

SAMUEL *mutters to himself.*

*Pause.*

*A fight breaks out outside. Noise filters in and* REG *tumbles through the door, yelling.*

REG

Bastard! [*He turns suddenly, sees* ZOË *at the bar and yells.*] That brother of yours is dead, Zoë. [*He wipes himself down and wanders over to the pool table.*]

JULIA

Poor ol' Reg. Having a hard day of it.


## Scene 4

BELINDA.

BELINDA

Why didn't you come in last night?

SAMUEL

Oh, got distracted. Ended up in Armadale. Had some good luck, and a bit of bad luck. One doesn't come without the other.

BELINDA

[*Spies* WILLIAM.] That's him – William, you're a bastard. [*To* SAMUEL.] Got any money left?

SAMUEL

Yeah, how much do you want? What's your problem with me mate Bill?

BELINDA

Bastard.

SAMUEL

How much do you want?

TAXI DRIVER *enters.*

TAXI DRIVER

Hey, you [*Points to* BELINDA.] where's my fare?

SAMUEL

How much?

TAXI DRIVER

Ten bucks.

SAMUEL *waves ten dollars at him.*

BELINDA

[*Violently.*] I don't want your fucking money!

TAXI DRIVER

Okay – you pay me.

BELINDA

I don't have anything to pay you with.

TAXI DRIVER

Okay, his money suits me fine. [*Snatches the ten dollars* SAMUEL *is sarcastically waving in the air.*]

*He leaves.*

BELINDA

Bastard.

SAMUEL

Have a drink. Meet my friends.

BELINDA

Friends be fucked. They're just sponging off you. And you let them. You disgust me. You're pissed and stupid. And as for William, he knows what happens when you get like this. He loves to see you like this. He pulls the wool over your eyes, you silly bastard. I'm sick of being left at home alone while you go on binges. Sick of it! Had William trying to break in last night whining that he needed a fuck. This is what I have to put up with from your friends.

SAMUEL

Sod off. I know you make things up. You just want to imprison me. I won't be held back. I have an obligation to go out and see what's happening in the world. It's my money, and I can spend it. I'm flush. Real flush at the moment. My horse came in you might say. Hit paydirt.

JULIA *and* ZOË

Yeah, sod off, Samuel's our friend. You're a stuck-up bitch.

SAMUEL

[*Bristles.*] Okay, guys, this is my business.

JULIA

[*Snidely.*] Okay then, boss.

BELINDA

[*Waving to* JULIA.] Yeah, boss! Got to get our little injection of excitement from somewhere – haven't we.

SAMUEL

[*Butts in.*] Being pissed might have something to do with this.

BELINDA

Apart from that. You're playing somebody else. Big shot. The guy with the bucks and power. Don't mean one thing you say. See what's happening in the world? You can't even see what's happening to your-self. Words are strangling you.

[*To the others.*] Listen, ladies, I live with this bastard. You probably see him every three months or so when he loses it. Well, let me tell you, he's no great guy. And as for the money, it's as much mine as his and to tell you the truth I'd never even give you the time of day let alone buy you a drink. And do you know what this big shot actually does for a living? I suppose he's told you he's a pilot or the son of station owner, or something equally grandiose and full of bullshit! Well, he's none of those. He's just a has-been school-teacher – thrown out for pissing it up on the job. He can't sleep at night because his dreams are too bright. He's a wreck. There's nothing to him anymore.

SAMUEL, *head hung low, puts his hands over his ears.*

ZOË
You're a first-rate bitch. Fuck off.

BELINDA *reaches over to* SAMUEL, *takes two one-hundred-dollar notes out of his pocket – she throws one at* JULIA *and takes the other to the bar.*

## Scene 5

BENNY.

*The* BARMAN *has left. A* BARMAID *is serving.* SAMUEL *is leaning a long way over the bar talking with her.* WILLIAM *is close to him, probably with an arm around him.* JULIA *and* ZOË *are absent.* BENNY *is sitting at a table on his own. At the table opposite sit* REG *and* JOE, *silent and watching* BENNY. BENNY *is balancing drink coasters and tapping his foot. This goes on for a couple of minutes.*

REG
Hey, Benny. What you doin'? Cat got ya' tongue?

REG *elbows* JOE *and they laugh.*

JOE

Yeah, Benny, cat got ya' tongue?

BENNY, *ignoring them, continues balancing coasters.*

BARMAID

[*Leaning past* SAMUEL.] Fuck off, Reg, leave him alone.

REG

What, you his sister are you?

JOE

Yeah, his sister!

REG

[*Elbowing* JOE.] More like his mother.

*They laugh.*

SAMUEL *gets up to move across to* REG. WILLIAM *tries to prevent him.*

WILLIAM

Now come on, Samuel, you're out of it here. It's none of your business.
Benny can look after himself.

SAMUEL

Let go.

WILLIAM

In fact Benny'd be angry if . . .

SAMUEL

Fuck off! That light's too bright. [*Motions to the* BARMAID.] Would you
mind turning it away from me, love, it burns. It's like lightning. [*She
does so, and he looks relieved.*]

SAMUEL *goes to* BENNY's *table, pulls out a chair and sits down, knocking* BENNY's *coaster-house down in the process.*

REG

Ha! Cool, Mr Smart-arse knocked Mrs Smart-arse's little house down.

SAMUEL

Sorry, Benny. [*Fumbles, trying to rebuild it.* BENNY, *motionless, merely watches him.*]

REG

Well, I wouldn't want to live in a house this Jack built.

*Laughter.*

SAMUEL

Fuck up and die!

REG *leaps up, knocking his chair over in the process.* WILLIAM *rushes over and stands behind* SAMUEL *who by now is sitting back with one finger raised.* BENNY *is still motionless.*

# Act 2

### Scene 1

*An alleyway running alongside the hotel.* REG *is bent over a person – a body – leaning up against a wall. It moves and we realize that it (*SAMUEL*) is semi-conscious.*

REG

[*Shaking* SAMUEL.] Come on, you bastard. Wake up.

SAMUEL

[*Incoherently.*] Thanks. I dreamt that I was being lifted high above the ground – claws of a nameless bird wrapped about my shoulders. I kept yelling, but no one could hear me. People seemed to be looking up in my direction, but could only see the bird.

REG

[*Punching and jabbing him now.*] Come on, you'll be all right.

SAMUEL

[*Comes to, in a fashion.*] Hell, yeah I'm all right. Just a bit out of it. Okay. Yeah. Here's your tip. [*Hands him $100. We might get the impression that the same bill is being exchanged.*] Okay. Now leave me alone.

REG *goes.*

SAMUEL

[*Rubbing his eyes, face.*] Fuck 'em. Got to pull myself together. Bad place to be. Ten slow deep breaths. Wow. Hyperventilating'll get me more out of it.

*[He tries to pull himself up using the wall but slides back down.]*

So this is what it comes to. A fuckin' alleyway next to the earliest opener and a syringe. What really makes me mad is the virtues one has to destroy to get here. It's a wet drought.

"to not be able to recall what has happened. To lose track . . . Ah, smack, the suppressor of ghosts, needer of corpses. Sweet, sweet . . . "

*[He tries to lift again but once again slides down.]*

Fuck Belinda. Doesn't she ever realize that I hate them but can't doing anything about it? She says I'm weak and I am. I know I'm weak.

"Unworthy though we men may be
Our Saviour Christ on Earth to see,
Kneel we here and pray that he
May grant us Heaven's crown."

I am a shepherd. I have watched then, watched them all . . . dance the dance of death. Here's my redneck refutation. I am not born of the country, though I go out there to drink, to wander from hotel to hotel and get away from you arseholes, you mob who've lost your way in this inner-city hell-hole:

I didn't connect regardless
how much I participated, it's a vocab thing
though not to do with skills of expression;
                                        ejecting bullets
from the breech, freezing whole carcasses
of home-slaughtered sheep, the contradictions
roll the same roads, and families
still come to visit:
                        crops in the bush, sullen days
coming down off bad speed, scoring from the old bloke
shacked up with teenage girls,
                                his bull terrier
crunching chickens;

a flat in the city is a deal
that can go either way, and the economics
of the paddock are the call-girl's profit;
                                    the ford fairmont
runs against the speed camera, and blind grass
poisons sheep – sightless like the minister
amongst his flock,
                          the school teacher,
                                    the father
who won't let his son play netball because it will turn him,
like an innocent bitten by a vampire, into a pervert – or worse —
   a poofter. Outside, you can't know that those
who speak in short, inverted sentences
always have fences in a state of disrepair,
                                    line length
and wire length are directly proportional,
eloquent subdivider of land, intensive pig farmer,
will let nothing in or out, though the space around the pig-shed
      is large and open, mainly used for hay cutting
while all sons play Guns 'n' Roses' "Appetite for Destruction",
timeless classic . . . apotheosis, serrated road edge
where a termite mound astoundingly remains intact: there
are no generics, no models of behaviour.
                          It's not that my
name is a misnomer: it's who owns                    ·
a particular conversation.

[*He laughs.*]


It's because I love too much. I know this to be the case. It's because I
can see how fucked up you all are.
Got to get it together!


*He manages to pull himself into a crouching position and begins to rock on his
haunches, whimpering.*

## Scene 2

WILLIAM

Come on, man, get it together.

SAMUEL

Yeah, I'm all right now.

WILLIAM

Then let's go. Get a cab. Get out of here.

SAMUEL

William, Belinda would be proud. [*With more solemn interlude.*] However, she'd say that this makes you more of an arsehole, that you've played at it for your own amusement as far as it will go. A voyeur. A predator.

WILLIAM

Come on, mate, you don't mean that.

SAMUEL

[*Leaping up suddenly, larger than life.*] PARASITE! Now fuck off and leave me in peace. I've been with the spirits and they're much better fuckin' company than sycophantic bastards like you.

[WILLIAM *leaves. Collapsing slowly and waveringly,* SAMUEL *adds . . .*]

. . . and at least they tell the truth, why even now they're saying,
   Samuel you're a fraud
   Samuel you're a fraud
   Samuel you're a fraud.

## Scene 3

JULIA *is crouched over* SAMUEL, *rubbing his chest.*

JULIA

Wake up, you horny bastard! You make me sick! What'd you say to
William? He's a mess. He's your mate – can't leave your mate. If you
don't stand by your mates then you're fucked.

[*Pause.*]

[*She slaps* SAMUEL.]

Wake up, you bastard or I'll piss on ya!

SAMUEL

I can hear you loud and clear. At the moment I'm trying to decide if
silence may not make my life more interesting.

*He pulls* JULIA *down and cuddles her. She laughs.*

JULIA

I like you, Samuel.

# Act 3

## Scene 1

*Public bar.* SAMUEL *is in alleyway.* WILLIAM *has just come back in. He goes straight to* JULIA.

JULIA

What's the problem? Reg?

WILLIAM

Yes. Well, no – not really. It's Samuel. Nobody else. It's what he wants. It's this crazy self-destructive bit he's into. He's just fine and then suddenly he's off. I follow him rather than accompany him. I mean, he asks me, and somebody's got to.

JULIA

Not to mention that he's good fun, spends heaps of dough, makes things happen. He's a pretty magnetic sort of person really.

WILLIAM

[*Smashing the table with a clenched fist and saying through gritted teeth.*] No, it's not that. I genuinely love him. He's special. Life would be so boring without . . .

ZOË

[*Who has appeared not to be listening.*] I reckon, Julia, that you're full of shit and it's you who takes him for a ride.

ZOË *leaves – goes and sits with the silent* BENNY *who has not moved.*

#### WILLIAM

What's with her?

#### JULIA

Don't worry about Zoë. She's a bit spun out about court. They'll put her away this time.

#### WILLIAM

What for?

#### JULIA

A bit of this, a bit of that.

#### WILLIAM

None of my business?

#### JULIA

You've got it. Anyway, how's Samuel?

#### WILLIAM

Basically an OD case. He's hanging in there. Nodding off, coming to.

#### JULIA

Okay, then. Normal.

*Pause.*

#### WILLIAM

[*Suddenly.*] This is the last time. I'm going to shake him for good. I'm not going to . . . assist him anymore. He's taking me, and Belinda for that matter, down with him.

#### JULIA

I don't think he's into Belinda very much. Maybe it's what's called "a marriage of convenience." She hates his friends, hates his wandering off. Hates his gambling, his fighting. She shouldn't worry – there'd be more to worry about if he ever won a fight. And she's always surrounded by her cronies. Sitting there and drinking sherry, bitchin' on about him because they couldn't get a fuck if they worked in a brothel.

WILLIAM

Don't kid yourself – she's the only person keeping him alive. She holds his esteem, self-respect.

JULIA

[*Laughs loudly.*] Sweet – he must have a lot of it if somebody "holds" it.

WILLIAM

No, he really loves her, is what I mean to say.

JULIA

Na, I know blokes like him. Sure, he's a bit smarter than most but I know what drives them. He doesn't love. He's like me. I don't love. We live to experience – to rob life of everything, to leave it empty and wasted behind us. It's all heroics.

WILLIAM

I can't believe in this. And I've known Samuel for years. He's not like that. And I don't think you are either.

JULIA *laughs, rubs his hair, and exits out front door.*


## Scene 2

REG *and* WILLIAM *playing pool.*

REG

Your mate's real weird.

WILLIAM

Yeah, I suppose he is.

REG

What, he's a school-teacher, eh?


WILLIAM

Yeah, supposed to be.


REG

Haven't seen him in here before this morning. Gave him a little taste this morning. Hungry bastard.


WILLIAM

He's been coming in about every two or three months for the last five years. Wanders round the countryside a fair bit. Works a bit here and there. Hay carting, penning sheep . . . that kind of thing. Always seems to come up with dough when things are tough.


REG

Yeah, well, I've only been in town for the last couple of months. I trust you, but I'm not sure about him. Did I mention that I'm Zoë's brother?


WILLIAM

[*Surprised.*] Yeah?


REG

[*Somewhat withering.*] Well, half-brother, anyway. She hates me. But family is family. And I'm older so she should respect me.


WILLIAM

[*Cautiously.*] Right.


REG

[*Unsure of whether or not he should have a go at* WILLIAM, *lets it hang but slams the white ball against his target with great ferocity.*] Hot shit!


*There is a long, uncanny pause. The* BARMAID *walks past and collects glasses. The* TWO POLICEMEN *walk in, perform a dance routine with their revolvers, and leave. Nobody reacts, or even appears to notice.*

If you don't sink a ball soon, I'll have you over the table. No, mate, watching you and your mate I think I might have to be careful what I say.

*He laughs hard, calls* JOE *over from the bar and repeats the joke to him softly – they laugh loudly.*

WILLIAM *continues to play.*

*Pause.*

REG

So what's the guy's problem?

WILLIAM

Samuel, I guess you mean?

REG

Yeah, the weirdo.

WILLIAM

He's all right, Reg. He's cool.

REG

Don't bullshit me.

WILLIAM

I suppose he's lonely.

REG

[*Throwing the pool cue onto the table.*] You can keep your pants, but you're a weak bastard.

## Scene 3

JULIA *and* SAMUEL *stagger through the door.* SAMUEL *goes to the bar, bangs a can, shakes it and sprays it over* WILLIAM. *The* BARMAN – *now back – reaches over the bar and grabs* SAMUEL *who throws a hundred-dollar note at him. The* BARMAN *retreats.* WILLIAM *wipes himself down. The others in the bar laugh – including* JULIA.


JULIA

Look, everybody, Willy's wet himself.


## Scene 4

SAMUEL *in movement, precipice, drops – space between steps etc.*

SAMUEL

[*To* JULIA.] Muybridge. He was this guy from England who went to America who ended up studying the movement of animals and humans. He wrote this long work. Maybe I've got it wrong. I'm not sure if he was from England, or ever went to England. He was just a photographer really who worked for this railway magnate. He wanted to prove that at a particular time all four legs of a trotting horse were off the ground. After taking loads of publicity shots and thinking real hard about it, our friend finally cracked it. He filled up twelve to twenty cameras, took photos at two frames a second and proved the theory right. Then he spent the rest of his fucking life taking photographs of animals and humans moving and showing them to people on a thing he called a zoopraxiscope. He took sequences of lions, tigers, kangaroos, naked women walking up and down staircases, gentlemen leapfrogging, crippled children walking on all fours. He drew diagrams and injected into the picture Greek, Roman and any other mythological reference he could. He shot, through movement, he established a total world view. In a sense his world was meaningless in itself, but he believed in it himself, his whole self; that gave it relevance. [*He semi-chants the following.*]

Lions, tigers, kangaroos . . .
Lions, tigers, kangaroos . . .
Lions, tigers, kangaroos . . .
Lions, tigers, kangaroos . . .

You're trying to cast a spell, aren't you? Everyone else here, except maybe for ol' Wet Willy over there, would say that's bullshit. Reg'd probably deck you for it. But me, I know the secrets, and I know you are making spells.

JULIA *leans over and kisses him on the forehead. She begins to dance to a tune on the silent jukebox. The dance should be circular and wind off in a spiral. It eventually concludes at the corner of the pool table where* BENNY *is about to make a shot. She stops behind him, takes his hat and puts it on her own head, and then over his eye as he makes his stroke.*

## Scene 5

SAMUEL
[*To* JOE.] What part of the country do you come from?

JOE
My people are from around Pinjarra . . .

SAMUEL
Reg and Zoë relatives?

JOE
They say they are my cousins, but I don't know, I just don't know. Maybe brothers, or sisters. I don't know, just don't know. My short-term memory is failing, and I haven't known them that long . . . You're pretty nosey, aren't you!

SAMUEL
Yeah, guess I am. Are you in love with Zoë?

JOE
Nope.

*There is an uncomfortable silence – all background music stops.* SAMUEL *pulls a book from his pocket and grows visibly more agitated as he flicks through the pages. He throws it across the bar and the* BARMAN *reacts violently, pulling a club out from behind the bar.*

BARMAN

I've just about had a gutful of your shit, mate. Never stops. You're fucking soft in the head. If you don't get out of here I'll beat the living crap out of you. One more scene like this and you'll be banned for life. I'm not fucking joking, so don't pull fucking faces at me! Fucking junkies! Somebody oughta give the lot of you hot shots. Waste you for fucking good!

*Lighting changes.* SAMUEL *becomes majestic, dangerous. All in darkness, only* SAMUEL *illuminated.*

SAMUEL

The Boylyagaduks have the Boylya power and take to the air with ease and pleasuring. They can be invisible, but not to other Boylyagaduks. We see each other, but none of the others we see can see us. They are in darkness. It is their night. At night we can enter them and eat them from the inside out. We will be the smashed glass that gets into the feet. Suitable footwear, it says up there, but we don't have shoes. They don't have shoes. We get inside, like quartz, like glass!!

*Blackout.*

## Scene 6

*Alleyway.* SAMUEL, REG, *and* WILLIAM.

REG

So this bloke's having some too, eh?

WILLIAM

Yes. He's buying.

SAMUEL

Yeah, he needs a lift.

REG *and* SAMUEL *laugh.*

REG

[*Handing something to* SAMUEL.] You oughta stick to the same shit, mate. It'll really screw you up mixing it like this. But it's your funeral, and as long as I get paid, why should I care? There you go, bloke, it's all yours. I'm clearing out for a while. Tomorrow, maybe. I hear you turn up every two or three months [*shoots a glance at* WILLIAM] – I'll probably be back by then.

*He leaves.*

SAMUEL

[*Sarcastically.*] Well, me boy, big moment for you. Sharing stuff with me again.

WILLIAM

[*Flatly.*] Yeah.

## Scene 7

SAMUEL

Hey, man, you've lost your sparkle. Last night at that club you had real sparkle – and in your tongue, words wither the bowels out of anyone. What's happened? Choke on the rosy-fingered dawn? Hey remember that time we swam across the river half-cut? Into the black waters of the river we went, swearing an oath of eternal friendship. That was before you shacked up with that chick who wouldn't have a bar of me. So much for oaths. Once out on the Avon, up near the salt lakes at Yenyenning, I saw the ghosts of men rise out of the carcasses of sheep. I said a prayer for them and they stared straight through me. I burnt the carcasses, and the smoke turned into storm clouds that broke open and filled the lakes, washing the salt down into the river system. What happened to you last night, Bill?

WILLIAM

Wouldn't know.

SAMUEL

Not going to get a bite out of you. Oh well, this should charge us both up.

SAMUEL *finds a clean surface, sets up the lines of speed using his cigarette box. Rolls a bill and snorts. Hands the bill to* WILLIAM.

WILLIAM

[*Snorts.*] Wow, what a rush . . .

*They both lean against the wall, looking skyward.*

# Act 4

## Scene 1

*Allegory. In the alleyway.*

*Speech is agitated, both are speeding.* WILLIAM *is pouring out a can of beer – in piecemeal jerks – as they are speaking. A kind of libation.*

WILLIAM
What are we doing here, Samuel?

SAMUEL
Waiting. I'm pinging. Want to wind down. I spoke to your bloke again and he said he's got something to slow me down. Always have a back-up plan. Lined this up a couple of days ago, have just been waiting for it to fall into place. Someone up there has been wrecking things for me lately, but I feel fortune will shine upon me – us – shortly. Maybe that Julia is good for me. Maybe . . . [*Pause.*] We're waiting . . .

WILLIAM
I hate to ask the obvious, but who . . . ?

SAMUEL
For Reg.

WILLIAM
For Reg? Again? When did you speak to him?

SAMUEL
A figure of speech. To put you off. He was just going to see a man about a dog. We communicated with a glance. In the end, he's the one

who'll think of me. Doesn't know you're my right-hand man. He's
scoring some wicked slow. You're on a need-to-know basis. Sometimes
whole lives are communicated in a glance. Need to sleep, need to get
back to the dream. Things to do, places to go, things to see. Need to
stop thinking about the cunning goddess, Belinda.


WILLIAM

You gave him money? When? I didn't see you give him any extra.


SAMUEL

Yeah, 250 for half a "g" and a 50-dollar tip. Sleight-of-hand. I saw him
in the meadows, running with the asphodel, a beast with a club. His
name is Orion, and he is the hunter of ghosts.


WILLIAM

[Insanely.] "Slow"? That's shit. I want some more quick. I want to get on
my dancing shoes and split this shit hole. I wanna get my aunty out
of it and play some music down at the Stoned Crow with her. I wanna
run faster than the crows can fly, I want to stay awake for days. I'm
flying. I wanna fly more. It feels great.


SAMUEL

Slow. What we all need – slow. Brain's been a bit hyperactive lately,
time to wind down and nod off. I've lost something. Something's
taken my power. Gotta get it back again. Go searching. Everything
seems clear on quick, but nothing really is. Thoughts can't catch up
with themselves. It's a facade.


WILLIAM

But why am I here? I am going nowhere, just around in circles, there
and back.


SAMUEL

Going over the same ground doesn't make things clearer.


WILLIAM

Yeah, but I don't see . . .

*[Loudly.]* Don't give me any crap here, O curious one. You drink the blood that will open your eyes. They bring powder into the country inside their bodies.

WILLIAM

Okay. Keep it down. You're speaking shit, mate. Too much fucking tequila. You're all messed up. I should give you a good thumping.

SAMUEL

Yeah, well . . .

*[Pause.]*

Hey, you reckon we've had a good time?

*[*WILLIAM *groans and* SAMUEL *laughs snidely to himself.]*

Wonder what Belinda's doing now?

WILLIAM

Probably at work.

SAMUEL

No way. She'll be on the phone to her mother or something all day. All fucking day. Witch.

WILLIAM

The cops wander past here all the time . . .

SAMUEL

You're right, she'll be at work cursing me under her breath wishing she had a mother to ring and say, "He's a bastard."

WILLIAM

You are, you know!

SAMUEL

Thanks.

[*Pause.*]

I haven't pissed all day. Those tequilas dried me up inside.

*Pause.*

WILLIAM

Do you think he'll come?

SAMUEL

I couldn't care less, to tell you the truth. I'll wait another ten minutes and then, fuck off. To tell the truth I'm pretty bored with all this now.

WILLIAM

[*Suspicious, even excited.*] Let's go now, Samuel. Even if he does come there'll only be trouble. I'm starting to spin out, mate.

SAMUEL

Now you've given me a good reason to stay.

## Scene 2

JOE *enters the alleyway and makes his way over to* SAMUEL *and* WILLIAM – *who remain unmoved.*

JOE

Hey, are you the wanker waiting for Reg?

SAMUEL

Maybe. "To pull down the fruit when the autumn comes . . . "

JOE

Yeah, you're them. The smart-arse and the quiet one.

SAMUEL

What do you want? I paid Reg.

JOE

I got the money but I'm giving the dope directly to you. I promised Reg's sister I wouldn't let him hold the dope. The cops have their eye on him.

SAMUEL

Ha, I've already got some off him today, so you haven't done too well.

JOE

It weren't from me. You look fried. Sure you want this?

*Pause – takes a packet out.*

SAMUEL

[*Feels the packet, tastes it.*] Gotta level out. Okay.

JOE

Got some picks?

SAMUEL

Reg usually carries a few fresh ones.

JOE

Fuck. I feel like a blast myself. Back in a minute – I'm off to the chemist for a fitpack.

SAMUEL

[*Agitated. Hanging out. Hyped up and waiting for a blast. Picks up an empty beer can and rips it in half.*] There. Substitute spoon.

*He then walks off stage and comes back balancing the half-can full of water.*

*They both sit and stare at the half-can, aware that it looks slightly ludicrous.*

*Long pause.*

#### WILLIAM

Enough fucking water in there to hit up the whole city. Won't the dirt from the serial number taint the water?

#### SAMUEL

[*Slumping his shoulders.*] Probably. Belinda has been sick. I have drawn the sickness out of her. [*Searches his pockets and take out something – maybe pieces of quartz or glass.*] The Boylyas.

*Long pause.*

JOE *appears.*

# Act 5

*Public Bar. Now dim, yellow light. Faint music in the background but it's not coming from the jukebox. Something dirge-like – though beyond definition. Maybe The Cult, Bauhaus . . . ? As* BENNY *speaks, the light reddens – when he finishes it yellows again.*

## Scene 1

*Benny Speaks.*

BENNY *is on his own again playing with coasters. Suddenly he lets out a long wail, scatters the coasters, jumps onto his seat, rocking on his haunches.*

### BENNY

I first come to this place eight years ago. I come here because one by one the city hotels work out ways to keep black people out. I come here and watch this place and learn to feel safe here. I come here in a hat and everyone says, "Hey; look at this dude – he's either cool or up himself."

[*Pause – he laughs.*]

But it doesn't cross their minds why I come here. Even my mates who come here for the same reason don't say it.

[*Pause.*]

What I want to say is – that fella Samuel – you don't like him – but he's all right. He come here once in a dress with a few hundred bucks. While he was buying the drinks nobody said anything but when he run out of dough a few fellas decked him. He lifted himself up, laughed, took off his dress and gave it to me sister.

[*Pause.*]

He was wearing jeans and a shirt underneath and asked me for a drink. I told him to go home and sleep it off.

[*Pause.*]

Another time he comes in here and gives everyone flowers. He gave me two and I crushed them in front of him. He tried to grab me around the waist but I said Wooo, don't think that stuff on me matey, or you're dead. He said okay, I'm dead.

[*Pause.*]

And I'll tell you something – I reckon that chick – Belinda – was some-one he met last night and paid to pull that stunt. And that mate of his, he knows all this and goes along with it! That's what I reckon.

[*Pause.*]

[*Singing.*] "The men were broken-hearted as they heard me, and threw themselves on the ground groaning and tearing their hair, but they did not mend matters by crying . . . She passed through the midst of us without our knowing it, for who can see the comings and goings of a god, if the god does not wish to be seen?"

[*Pause.*]

[*Begins to wail.*]

[*The* TWO POLICEMEN *walk in, look around, go to the bar and speak with the* BARMAN *who comes from off stage. The* BARMAN *hands them two dresses. They put these on and go and stand on either side of* BENNY.]

And I'll tell you something else —

*[At this moment the police grab, blindfold, and handcuff him – he is led out the doors.]*

I tell you, that Samuel is dying. Some people reckon he kills the spirit of his friends. He thinks of himself as a great host, but some don't see it this way. They say he'll pay for it. Pay for his in-your-face attitude. But when he speaks it is glorious to me. Glory glory glory!

## Scene 2

*The Dance.*

JULIA *and* ZOË *repeat* SAMUEL's *Muybridge soliloquy then begin a spiralling dance. The dance winds out, consuming all. The dance is to be culturally "relevant" to the place of performance. Ironic, but respectful, as if respect is all there is left to hold things together. The mock solemnity is really genuine hope.*

## Scene 3

REG

*[To* JULIA.*]* Hey, the fucker's had too much!

JULIA

Piss off!

REG

*[Grabbing her.]* Hey, I mean it!

*They exit and return in a short while with* SAMUEL. JULIA *is slapping him around the face,* REG *is holding him.*

JULIA

Sit him here – up against the wall. He's fucked! Really fucked. Come on, babe, come on. Pull ya shit together. Don't fucking die on me, you bastard! You fucking bastard!

### SAMUEL

[*Snaps out of it briefly, exclaims the following, half-consciously but with a frenetic intensity. . . .*] When I walk outside my body the electricity in the air makes me sleepy, I have to fight to stay awake. It's the lightning. The lightning comes and I can barely keep my eyes open. It's blinding. I was walking along a country road a few years ago – way out where the wheat is thin-headed and the crop never grows tall, when a storm rolled in and set the world alight. There were few trees to ground the strikes and I was a beacon. I went low to the ground and the time between thunder and the torn metal of the strike decreased. It struck near by me, and the ground shook. The rain pelted down. Soaked to the skin I grew sleepy, and slept into the next day. A farmer woke me there on the side of the road. You don't look so good, matey, he said. I told him about the lightning and he left me to walk the ten miles to town alone. [*He searches his pockets.*] They've gone! They've gone! What have I done with them! They are the bad people I've been, removed, made into quartz. Don't let them escape, don't let then loose! Watch the eagle, watch it over Narrogin, high over the town. Or further West . . .

Seen briefly over Wallaby Hills
it distorts the way we witness
errors in a fenceline, patches
where sheoaks work the southerly
outside science. Immense,
it stabilises before going
with the currents, making cold air
productive, and small animals
carrion on our event
horizon. Hakeas fibrillate
and charges of stamens fall
in brushes, yellow magnetic,
wires charging up to the heavyweight:
uplifted overhead.

*He convulses, then lapses back into a coma, the others shaking him, trying to walk him about.*

JULIA

Walk him! Keep him moving. [*They struggle with him. She checks his pulse.*] It's stopped! there's nothing there! Nothing at all.

REG

But he's smiling. Look at the bastard, he's smiling!

# Act 6

## Finale

*The entire cast recites the following as a strophe/anti-strophe structure. The arrangement is at the director's discretion though a "sing-song" structure is most effective. This should be an "over the top" revue-like scene, reminiscent of cabaret.*

*Strophe.*

> And fare ye well, each worthy friend;
>> May God his mercy show now.
> For here at last we make an end.
>> Farewell! From you we go now.

*Anti-Strophe.*

> What moral autonomy remains
>> As from frame to frame he walks ...
> From town to town, searching out
>> Brothers and sisters, scattered about ...

THE END

## Preface

Collections of unpublished plays by John Kinsella are held in the National Library of Australia, the Scholars' Centre at Reid Library, University of Western Australia, and more recent manuscripts are held in the Kenyon Library, Ohio, USA. The National Library of Australia has drafts of a play called *The Chimney Sweep*, as well as *The Eyes*, among others. The Scholars' Centre at Reid Library, UWA, holds drafts of *Paydirt*, and extracts from *The Shooting Party* and *Crop Circles*. Some material at the Reid Library is still to be processed, and play drafts in the National Library of Australia may not have been recognized as such. Researchers, and/or directors are advised to peruse the website: Guide to Australian Literary Manuscripts (http://findaid.library.uwa.edu.au). My thanks to Dr Toby Burrows of the Scholars' Centre, UWA, for this information.

## Crop Circles

The author offers a special thank you to Carla Zampatti, for her support with this play.

*Crop Circles* first appeared as print text in the journal *imago* (13.2) 2001, published by University of Queensland Press. The contents of this issue can be found at:
http://www.imago.qut.edu.au/issues/13.2/contents.html.

Sayers drives a *Statesman*. This particular make of Australian car, by General Motors Holden, was, and still is a popular car of choice for farmers and rural dwellers – although the four-wheel drive invasion has impacted on its popularity. Modelled on North American cars of the 1970s and 80s – with a big 5 litre V8 motor – they are ideal for country cruising, although a bit cumbersome for city parking. They are relatively large, relatively luxurious, and can handle large potholes in the roads, bales of hay in the boot, a sheep or two in the back seat – and do service with a wash and polish as a symbol of prosperity at the race meeting, and polo match.

*Round up.* A brand name for a variety of weedkiller, very popular in the bush and the suburbs – where, in the latter environment, with a handheld squirtgun, any invading flora can be dispatched with a blast of "round up" to permeate its leaves, and kill it all the way down to its roots.

Gary, the shearer, wears *greasies.* Often a name applied to shearers in general, it comes from their clothes being impregnated with the lanolin from the fleeces of sheep. Here, it refers to a style of trousers worn by shearers.

Figure 1: The set under construction.

Figure 2: Act 1, Scene 3. Wright shovels, and Mary plants trees under the watchful eye of the Greenie.

Figure 3: Act 2, Scene 4. The minister preaches "The Song of Solomon".

Figure 4: Act 4, Scene 2. The trees are planted.

## *Smith Street*

This script was published in *Mudlark: An Electronic Journal of Poetry & Poetics* 19, 2002. This site can be accessed at:
http://www.unf.edu/mudlark/mudlark19/contents.html

*Wowsers* are a feature of this play, specifically in the character of Mrs Walpurgis. Mr Clipboard appears to have his own agenda, but is characteristic in his empirical notation of wrong-doing. Wowsers are characterized by their enjoyment in curtailing the real or imagined pleasures of others. The practice, if not the word has had long currency in Australia. Other nations have their own variations of these moral police.

Figure 1: Act 1, Scene 2. "Do I know you?"

Figure 2: Act 1, Scene 4. "Spitting on your sort."

Figure 3: Act 1, Scene 4. "Cut the crap."

Figure 4: Act 2, Scene 1. "You're a man's man. A blokey bloke."

Figure 5: Act 2, Scene 4. "One more crack and that's it."

Figure 6: Act 3, Scene 1. "The city is a body. The body eats itself."

Figure 7: Act 3, Scene 3. "Every womb is sacred."

Figure 8: Act 3, Scene 4. "An apparation of the Virgin."

# Paydirt

John Kinsella writes: "This play is intended to undo stereotypes through the irony that can never be divorced from the artifice that is the stage. It was originally written for the brilliant Nyungar actor, David Ngoombujarra, though it was never shown to him. Many of the characters in this play have their inspirations in a fractured group of people I spent much time with. This is a work of respect. No player in the play is specifically black or white, regardless of what other characters say of them or describe them as. The boundaries are fluid. Land should be returned – without limitations – to the rightful custodial owners of 'Australia' – the indigenous peoples."

For the Strophe, see Alexander Franklin's *Seven Miracle Plays* (London: Oxford Univ. Press, 1979), "The Shepherds" for his modern English rendering.

For the Anti-Strophe, see Samuel Butler's translation of *The Odyssey*, Book X. London: Longmans, Green & Co., 1900.

*Boylyagaduks*. Samuel's lines describe what these "spirit" manifestations can do. When they inhabit their host, they feel like sharp pieces of quartz grinding in the bodies of their "victims". See Sir George Grey's *Vocabulary of the Dialects of South-Western Australia* (London: T. & W. Boone, 1840).

# BIBLIOGRAPHY

Franklin, Alexander. *Seven Miracle Plays*. London: Oxford University Press, 1979.

Grey, George, Sir. *Vocabulary of the Dialects of South-Western Australia*. 2nd ed. London: T. & W. Boone, 1840.

Homer. *The Odyssey*. Trans. Samuel Butler. London: Longmans, Green and Co., 1900.

*Imago: New Writing* (13.2) 2001.

Mengham, Rod and Glen Phillips, eds. *Fairly Obsessive: Essays on the Works of John Kinsella*. Fremantle Western Australia: Centre for Studies in Australian Literature/Fremantle Arts Centre Press, 2000.

*Mudlark: An Electronic Journal of Poetry & Poetics* 19, 2002. This site can be accessed at <http://www.unf.edu/mudlark/mudlark19/contents.html>

Printed in the United Kingdom
by Lightning Source UK Ltd.
9701300001B/1-3